BLACK
Like You

Published by MME Media
First published by MME Media in 2012
MME Media (South Africa), PO Box 1637, Gallo Manor 2052
Johannesburg, South Africa
www.mmemedia.co.za

ISBN: 978-0-620-45686-9

Edited by Lynda Gilfillan
Proofread by John Linnegar
Cover Design by Adam Rumball, Sharkbuoys
Typeset by Sharkbuoys, Johannesburg
Cover photograph by Siphiwe Nkosi
Printed and bound by Ultra Litho (Pty) Limited

BLACK Like You

HERMAN MASHABA
An Autobiography

By Herman Mashaba
and Isabella Morris

MMEmedia

Foreword
by Dikgang Moseneke

The most abiding feature of the human condition is, perhaps, storytelling. Some stories are tales that we tell simply to amuse ourselves around the fireside. But other stories are meant to do more. They seek to do what the African idiom describes as *ukuzilanda*. In its essence, the idiom carries the notion of going back in time and painstakingly, but proudly, recounting one's roots. Each one of us has a lineage and connectedness with our immediate and ancient forebears, our siblings, the village or neighbourhood that nurtured us, the traditional or formal schools we went to, as well as with the partners we met, and loved, and with whom, perhaps, we brought offspring into the world. We are also connected to the career choices we made along the way.

However, the somewhat predictable trajectory along which most lives unfold, disguises the social and political context that conditions how we live. It may blind us to the personal and public scorn that may have been tolerated along the way. It may hide the gritty resolve one needs to make choices, set goals and achieve them. When we look at them closely, however, many stories demonstrate that life is never linear, but instead varied and complex. A life story confronts us with the rich and textured social context within which personal grief and triumph unfold.

On the other hand, a story may be told as an affirmation of one's own self and one's societal worth. It may be a public testimony of a life well lived, a life that is worth recounting.

Even so, good storytelling has an intrinsic worth well beyond its motive. That, perhaps, is what motivated Herman Mashaba in *Black Like You* to emulate his forebears. He seems to have succumbed to the instinct of *ukuzilanda* – retracing his steps, and asking crucial questions: "How did I arrive here?" and "What was it all about?"

In the 25 years I have known Herman, I have seen him live much of the story he tells. I first met him when he was a young, struggling entrepreneur, and I admired the fact that he had the guts to take on the system in those dark days of apartheid. When I look at what he has achieved, despite the odds, I know the answer to the question as to how he arrived where he is today. Over the years, I have been a friend, but also an elder brother to Herman; I have listened to his ambitions, encouraged him on his journey, and I continue to admire all his achievements – including this autobiography.

Of course, once one assumes the onerous task of writing one's own life story, as Herman Mashaba does in *Black Like You*, the first challenge is that of candour. An autobiography is as much an insightful retreat into the past as it is a wide-ranging revelation. Herman's account is rather like looking at oneself in a full-length mirror – but then the perennial challenge to an autobiographer sets in. The writer must confront the reflection and describe the warts and blemishes; but there is also beauty, and even magnificence in the image. On this score, *Black Like You* fares admirably on both counts. Herman does not shy away from the uneasy details of his undiscerning youth, and yet he does take a bow for well-deserved bouquets in his later life.

Going beyond the rural confines of Herman's early years, the story develops into a riveting tale that remains centred on his family. Herman had a deep love for his mother, and presents her as a heroine who was dealt a bad hand by history. We can almost see his face light up as he tells the tale of the lifelong love between himself and Connie, the wife he admires and cherishes. He remembers with fondness his optimistic grandfather insisting that he be named "Highman", a name which mutated into "Herman". Also, he has kind words for the sister who stepped in as his surrogate mom. Perhaps the most wrenching account is his complex, emotional relationship with his brother, and the latter's untimely passing.

Herman Mashaba's personal account is enhanced by the recurring theme of the social and political struggles fought in our country. By the time Herman had moved to the more urbanised township of Temba for his high school education, he had become alert to the spreading youth revolts in urban schools and universities. To a large extent, this explains his brief and abortive stay at the University of the North.

We learn that, from a young age, Herman displayed a clear sense of personal worth. He would sooner starve that submit to menial and demeaning gardening piece-jobs offered over weekends in racist white households at the time. He was blessed with ample native common sense, and he bore a youthful blowtorch that cut through every hurdle that stood in his way. Moreover, he knew that in the end he had to start his own business and thus create a job for himself and also for others.

The genesis of that remarkable business, Black Like Me, is a study in sheer ingenuity and tenacity. The respective roles of Herman and Connie, and indeed other partners in the business, are recounted with detailed precision; but there is tension, too, in the tale. The fire that gutted the historic black-owned factory was as devastating as it was daunting. Yet Black Like Me rose like a phoenix from the ashes of that fire. This commercial struggle took place within the inestimably unjust constraints placed on black entrepreneurs by colonialism and apartheid. It is as well to add that Black Like Me shone beacon-like amidst the indescribable social ruin experienced by oppressed black people.

Herman and Connie Mashaba have been widely acknowledged and honoured for a job exceptionally well done. Herman lectures on business leadership globally, and also at home. Even more admirably, in South Africa he coaches, mentors and financially supports many young entrepreneurial hopefuls. A better role model, truer patriot and son of the soil I can hardly imagine. At a time when somewhat limited and even rapacious young business leaders descend on the trough of public tenders, our youth would do well to read *Black Like You*. Our continent, Africa, more than any other, deserves patriotic, honest and competent business leaders who, like Herman Mashaba, may proudly retrace their roots and recount the details of their lives.

Dikgang Moseneke, Deputy Chief Justice of South Africa

Introduction
by Herman Mashaba

When is the right time to write an autobiography? Some people may think that the right time is when you've lived a full life. Well, certainly, my life has been filled with experiences that range from the ordinary to the outrageous, sorrowful to joyful, easy to difficult. But even these experiences, for me, weren't the qualifying criteria for writing my story. Nor was it the constant pleas – "Herman, when are you going to write a book about your life?" – that made me sit down and put pen to paper.

What finally spurred me on to write was when I realised that my life experiences might, in some small way, help people to realise that there is a way out of difficult circumstances. My initial financial success came from my company, Black Like Me, but I am Black Like You and I believe that I understand the difficulties encountered by young black people.

This is my story; it is not motivated by ego, nor is it a veiled opportunity to ramble on about the successes I have achieved. I have abundant contact with young South Africans whose lives are difficult and challenging, and when I encounter their frustration and despair, I realise that I have a responsibility to help where I can. Though there are many upliftment and mentoring projects that I am involved in, these do not give me sufficient access to the many people who are in need of guidance.

My life is not a big life; in fact, nowadays it is a very ordinary, though privileged, one. But it wasn't always so. Like many young South African men and women, I grew up in a home where parental supervision was absent. I drank, gambled, womanised, took drugs, and even sold drugs in the formative and vulnerable years of my life. I know that this lifestyle was the norm for many youngsters growing up in the townships, and that it continues to be so for many young people today. However, nobody is telling this kind of story, so the misguided and unguided youth of today have no way of knowing that, no matter how deprived their lives are, there is a way out of it all, that they have the power to change the course of their lives.

I am convinced that I was born to be an active participant in life rather than a mere spectator. I believe that my grandfather recognised this, that my mother and sisters saw this potential, and that my life became a life worth living because of their faith in me. Their constant support and encouragement fuelled me to live the best life I could.

There are many people who feel that they have nobody who is there for them, that there is no one who will recognise and nurture their potential. I hope that my book will enable them to discover ways of recognising opportunities that will help them see a glimmer in the darkness, to find courage to step out into the light and live meaningful lives.

This book would not have been written without the support and encouragement I received from the following people: my wife and life partner, Connie, who has not only encouraged me, but loved me throughout our marriage; Moky Makura, my publisher, who insisted that my story had relevance to other South Africans, and persevered until I had no defence against her persistent nudging; writer Isabella Morris, who committed my words to paper; my children, Nkhensani and Rhulani, who continue to support me in my efforts, and my sisters, who have always believed in me. To all of you, I say thank you.

Herman Mashaba

Chapter 1

The headlights of oncoming cars illuminated the gravelly shoulder of the road where I was standing; shattered glass and mangled bits of metal glinted, a pool of radiator water gleamed. A woman in the crowd of onlookers told me, "An ambulance has taken the bodies, there was a lot of blood. But now we hear that the ambulance broke down on the way to the hospital."

A fist of dread tightened in my chest – was my brother Pobane among those injured bodies?

Hours earlier, I had received the news of Pobane's accident. I'd immediately left my home in Ga-Rankuwa and driven about a hundred and fifty kilometres along the busy road leading to Marble Hall. Now, I stood staring in disbelief at the wreckage of my brother's bakkie on the tar road outside Bela-Bela; this was the same light delivery vehicle that I had bought him to start his curtain and carpet fitment company just a few months before.

Pretoria's Steve Biko Hospital was closest to the scene of the accident, but at the time it was reserved for white patients only, so my brother was sent to Kalafong Hospital in Atteridgeville. The road to the hospital seemed a thousand kilometres long, and as my wife Connie and I drove there, we had no need for conversation; instead, we prayed that God had spared Pobane from death's clutches.

The woman at the scene of the accident had told us that another ambulance had been summoned from Pretoria, and that it had taken almost two hours to arrive. I hoped that Kalafong had the necessary expertise and equipment to attend to Pobane's injuries. Would the extra distance and the delay mean the difference between life and death for my brother? I tried to banish these thoughts from my head as we raced to the hospital.

The hospital's emergency entrance flickered red in the rotating light of a nearby ambulance. Doctors, nurses and anxious relatives darted between the reception area and the wards, and Connie and I were led to a waiting area. Standing in the bleak waiting room with its hushed conversations, where the smell of sickness and sterility vied for supremacy, I didn't want to hear what the doctor coming towards us was going to say. Connie, sensitive to my fears, slipped her hand in mine and squeezed it while the doctor consulted his clipboard. I closed my eyes; I had seen the car – or what was left of it – and found it hard to believe that anyone could have survived in the wreckage. Pobane and four of his co-workers and their carpeting and curtains and tools had all been in the bakkie, and I could only imagine the bedlam in that vehicle as it rolled – the confusion, the shouts, the screams of pain as they all tumbled about, and tools and materials and bodies slammed into each other.

"Mr Mashaba, I'm afraid that I don't have good news for you," the doctor said. I gripped Connie's hand tighter. "Your brother is in a critical condition. Unfortunately, he has sustained severe spinal injuries and, if he's lucky enough to pull through this precarious period, his chances of ever walking again are slim."

In spite of the doctor's grim prognosis, relief coursed through my body – Pobane had made it. I would not have to face my mother or my sisters to tell them that Pobane was dead; I would not have to stand in front of Pobane's wife, Salome, and their beautiful, wide-eyed young children and tell them that Pobane would not be coming home.

I was so grateful that God had spared Pobane that I visited him in Kalafong every day, ferrying his wife and children there and back, as well as my mother and sisters. I was so thankful that

Pobane was alive that I did not even contemplate what it might be like if he had to spend the rest of his life in a wheelchair. But my relief was short-lived, and a week later Pobane's condition deteriorated and he passed away. I felt doubly angry and sad – Pobane had survived the car tumbling through the air and landing in a twist of metal, he had survived the delayed journey to the hospital, how could he die now? It was a devastating blow. And, at the end of it all, I did have to stand in front of our grief-stricken family, comforting them and trying to reassure them that things would turn out okay. It was a terrible blow to my mother, losing a son she'd been so close to. And I felt enormous sadness for Salome, who was like a sister to me; she had lost her husband and her family's breadwinner, and she now faced the stress of having to support her young family.

On the cool spring day of Pobane's funeral, I battled to come to terms with his death. Pobane was just forty-five years old; I was only twenty eight. Why did I have to endure this loss at a time when everything else in my life seemed to be going well? My company, Black Like Me, was only three years old, but it was already soaring beyond my wildest dreams; why, then, did my brother have to be taken at such a time? Pobane and I had grown up in the same family, yet our lives had taken very different paths; my star was on the rise, and my brother's had been snuffed out. As I travelled across the sandy roads of GaRamotse to the funeral, bumping over streets that Pabone and I used to run along as bare-footed boys, I found myself wondering about the forces that shape our lives. How did it happen that two young men from the same family – who'd waved greetings to the same neighbours, attended classes in the same wonky school desks, and hidden behind the same trees to avoid being caught by the farmer we stole wood from – how had we come to embark upon two completely different life paths?

Throughout the years, at the conferences I have attended and at the workshops that I have hosted, people have asked me the question that I have asked myself a thousand times – what makes one man succeed and another man fail? This question has always resonated with me, because it is the question I have continually asked myself, especially when it comes to making sense of my brother's short life and contemplating my own full one.

I have so often asked myself the question: Could Pobane's life have had a different outcome? This I will never know, but what I can do is describe the unfolding of my own life.

I was born on the 26th of August 1959 in GaRamotse in Hammanskraal, about thirty kilometres north of Pretoria. A late winter wind blustered through the streets of the village on the day my mother went into labour with me, her fifth child. My life had begun like that of many, many young black South Africans. GaRamotse was a typically rural village, so remote and insignificant that, at the time, it did not even warrant a mention in any official maps. But while the village may have had no significant meaning to anyone other than the close community that lived within its boundaries, to the Mashaba family, my family, GaRamotse was the centre of our universe.

GaRamotse was one of many villages and townships that formed part of the greater Hammanskraal area. Among these were places such as Majaneng, Leboneng and Temba, where I lived at various times; I knew them all well, as my family moved around over the years. Such villages were generally drab, uninteresting places; the red earth of the dirt roads formed muddy canals in the rainy summer months, and in winter the roads were corrugated sandy strips overhung with whitened grass and the peeling branches of bluegum trees. In early autumn, though, the roadsides were brought to life by wild cosmos flowers that briefly bloomed pink, purple and white. Groups of modest mud homes huddled together amidst dense bushveld that, in summer, smelt sweet after afternoon thundershowers.

My mother and father, Mapula and Silas Matinte Mashaba, were an unconventional couple. In the 1950s it was uncommon for young black couples to go away and live apart from the extended family. Custom and financial circumstances usually meant that a young couple lived with the husband's family. But after her marriage, my mother felt that living with her in-laws would curb her spirit of independence, so she and my father kept a small house near his family home. By all accounts, my mother Mapula was an exceptionally independent young woman. She had excelled during her limited schooling, and as a young married woman she confided in her good friend and neighbour, Mrs Ramaphoko, that she wanted to go out to work.

My father worked as an assistant at Osbourne Pharmacy in Marshall Street, in Johannesburg. Whenever my older sisters, Esther, Florah and Conny, developed a fever or a touch of stomach trouble, my father's experience at the pharmacy helped him to concoct a mixture to cure their ailments, and, as a special treat, he often bought them lipstick. But for black women, at the time, there were far fewer opportunities. The only job my mother ever managed to find away from home was that of domestic worker – the bleak fate of many talented black women during the apartheid era.

To this day, my family and neighbours love to recount how important my birth was to my grandfather; for in the late fifties, it was an unusual cultural activity for men to be involved in what they considered women's business.

The day I was born, the wind sprayed sand through the village. But my grandfather closed his eyes against the sting of it as he rolled a twenty-five-litre drum down the road to the village dam. He took long strides, his body leaning into the wind, hoping, as he hurried, that my grandmother had lit a fire so that he could boil some water on his return. On any other day, my grandfather might have taken his time on the two-kilometre walk to the dam, stopping to roll a cigarette with a villager or accepting a mug of beer from a neighbour. But on that day he had to hurry because his daughter-in-law, my mother, was in labour, and my grandfather wanted to make sure that there was enough warm water for the birthing process and to wash the newborn baby.

Wisps of smoke trailed from village fires as the cold wind whipped bare flesh; village dogs limped towards the warmth of the flames, competing with children, who stood dancing from one foot to the other as they warmed their frozen hands. My grandfather gave a wave to neighbours who shouted greetings, apologising for his haste. Men usually steered clear of broad-hipped midwives and bosomy matrons who bustled about the mother in labour, for men had no business wincing at the sharp cries of a woman bringing a child into the world. But my grandfather puffed out his chest and told everyone he met along the way that his grandson was about to be born, and he didn't have time to indulge in small talk.

As he rolled the heavy drum up the road towards his home, my grandfather saw the glow of the fire and nodded with satisfaction. Without fanfare, he heated up the pots of water on an outside fire. There, he sat with my father, until, an hour or two later, a midwife put her head round the door and called my father inside the house. Shortly afterwards, my father emerged from the doorway and sat next to my grandfather at the fire.

"It's a boy," my father said, unable to conceal his pride. My grandfather nodded.

"I knew it would be a boy," he replied.

The two men stood at the fire and discussed names, as was their right. But it was my mother and father who had decided that their baby son would be called Samtseu, an ancestral name, and Philip, after a community clergyman.

"This is no ordinary boy, Silas," my grandfather said to my father. "This boy must have a name that will tell everyone that he will grow up to be an important man."

Although I had an older brother and three sisters, my father did not dare challenge my grandfather by insisting that all of his children were special, that they might all grow up to be influential. To this day, it is customary for age to be associated with wisdom, and it would have been discourteous to be dismissive of an elder's suggestion.

"His name will be Highman," my grandfather insisted.

I often wonder what my father thought at the time about my grandfather's grand vision. How did he manage to stop himself from dissuading my grandfather from giving me this strange name, with its connotations of highborn nobility and influence? My father had travelled further than GaRamotse, he had been to Pretoria and Johannesburg; my father knew only too well the absolute denial of status that black men suffered in the cities of South Africa. The villagers may have been somewhat protected from the direct, demeaning consequences of living under apartheid, but my father was under no illusion. Or, perhaps, did my father imagine a time when South Africa would be a democratic country and it would not matter whether you were a High Man or a Low Man, a time when everyone would enjoy the same rights? I am sceptical of the latter scenario, because even as I was growing up, and discussed political events with my friends and family, I never honestly believed that I would see democracy in my lifetime.

There are times I used to wish that my father had stood up to my grandfather, because growing up with a lofty name set me apart in some way from my peers. After soccer games that ended in dispute, I would have been overlooked in the fracas if my name had been Philip or Samtseu, but Highman just couldn't be ignored. Inevitably, my name was the butt of jokes, and even though I managed to shrug off the teasing, I grew up resenting this grandiose label. Fortunately, I was saved from eternal embarrassment when, as a young adult, I came across the name Herman and realised it would be easy enough to make a change. Herman was more ordinary and my friends had no trouble adopting it, even though there are some old-timers in the village who still call me Highman whenever I visit. It was only in post-apartheid South Africa that I legally changed my name to Herman when I applied for an identity document – a positive change in a positive political environment.

When I was two years old, my father died suddenly after a very short illness; I was too young to have any memories of him. Regrettably, my father never lived long enough for me to pour him a beer and ask him why he'd allowed people to call me by that unfortunate name, for he'd in fact officially registered the names my mother and he had chosen for me – Philip Samtseu.

My father's sudden death brought about drastic changes in the family – my mother had now become the family breadwinner. Like most villagers, my parents had enjoyed little more than a few years at school – generally, rural people had about three to five years of very basic education. So, in spite of my mother's obvious aptitude, her skills were limited to rearing a family, being a housekeeper, a wife, a mother, with all the attendant duties. There were few well-paid employment opportunities for her near the village and she was forced to do what millions of other black wives, sisters, aunts, mothers and grandmothers did: she looked beyond the village for a job that would provide her with an income to support her four children – my three older sisters and me.

During this early stage of my life, my brother, Pobane, who was seventeen years my senior, had already left home and was living independently. He had completed the minimum requirement school-leaving certificate, which was the equivalent of today's Grade 8. Our family considered this an important achievement, and had encouraged him to continue with his education. But Pobane had always been a reluctant student and, fearing that my parents would force him to continue studying, he had run away to Pretoria.

Fragmented families were a common feature of rural life as many people went to the cities to find work, and the Mashaba family was no different. By now it was the early sixties, and like many young black men Pobane had left his village to find fortune on city streets. Life was difficult enough for black men at the time, but it was even more difficult for those who did not have any skills. Unfortunately, Pobane was at the time one of thousands of unskilled workers in Pretoria.

Years later, as we matured and the age gap between us decreased, I got to know Pobane a bit better. I enjoyed the lively conversations we had, and I was sorry that he had not finished school; the opportunities, skills and knowledge that he would have gained, underwritten by maturity, might have allowed him to lead a much easier life.

Shebeens were the social hotspots for men in the townships. They mushroomed on the outskirts of Pretoria, where Pobane hung out. Thousands of men's lives ended in those shebeens before they'd even had a chance to get started. Long before they had even had the chance of tasting the fruits of hard work, they became addicted to the anaesthetising effects of alcohol. It helped them to forget their responsibilities and the demands their families made on them, and after a couple of drinks they could quickly forget that they'd been turned down for half a dozen jobs in a week, and that their wives in the village needed money for school fees for the children. Unlike many men who found that alcohol masked their disappointment, Pobane simply loved to socialise, and couldn't resist downing a couple of pints with his friends. In this way, we were similar – we both loved socialising. However, even that social indulgence affected his performance, and so Pobane managed to secure only temporary, poorly paid piece jobs that he happened to hear about from his network of friends and family. There were so many unskilled young black men looking for work that white employers had their pick of the bunch; they exploited the over-supply of employees who were willing to work for nothing more than their next meal.

With my brother living elsewhere, my sisters Esther, Florah, Conny and I lived alone, though I considered my relatives as part of the extended community in which I lived. In those days, it was accepted that a community looked after all the people who formed part of the community; that is how discipline was maintained, and that is how attention and care were given to those who needed it. This spirit of caring, within and by a community, is the real meaning of ubuntu.

Chapter 2

A home holds a family together, but unfortunately we did not own the house we lived in; my father died before he'd managed to save enough money to buy the materials needed to build a family home. After his untimely death, my maternal grandfather called the family together and collectively they decided that my sisters and I would live in my maternal great aunt's house, a short distance from my grandparents' home. They would be able to keep an eye on us there.

It was a modest home, constructed from mud, plastered on the outside, with a zinc roof, though without a ceiling. Zinc roofs were hell when the weather was extreme; during the searing months of summer we sizzled, and in the frosty months of winter we shivered. When we dressed in the mornings, our breath blasted white from our mouths as we chattered to one another. As I grow older, the discomforts and inconveniences of a difficult childhood seem less severe, as the warmth and intimacy my family enjoyed casts a glow on my memories. As a result, I look back on that time with increasing affection.

Because difficult economic circumstances in the villages forced many people to work in the cities, at least one parent was usually absent from the family. Our family was quite unusual, though, as we lived in a house without the presence of either of our parents to take care of us. It concerns me that this situation is still a frequent occurrence in South Africa in spite of improved economic opportunities – but today it appears to have less to do with economics and more to do with the devastating effect of HIV and AIDS on the family unit. Tens of thousands of AIDS orphans are forced to live without the care and supervision of their parents or older generations, having to rely on other children in the family to provide the necessary family support.

In our family, where neither father nor mother was present, the running of the home was left to my formidable sisters: Esther, Florah and Conny. Even though Pobane was working – albeit in just a temporary job – he neither contributed to nor placed any demands on the household. And, of course, once he had married Salome, he had an obligation to her and their children. His sporadic earnings were in any case barely sufficient to support his own family, let alone allow him to make a financial contribution to the care of his four siblings.

As challenging as it was for us to grow up without the presence of our mother, I can imagine that life was equally hard for her to be away from her children. The 1960s was the era of women's liberation in the western world, and many white South African women took advantage by staking their claim in the workplace, handing over their domestic and child-rearing duties to black housekeepers. My mother was one of millions of black women who worked as a housekeeper for a white family. When I consider how capable my sisters were in rearing me, I can only think that my mother would have been an asset to any family. I believe that my sisters' gentleness, their attention to maintaining a clean and orderly home, as well as their patience and fortitude, could only have been learnt from my mother's example during those rare times when she found work close enough to be able to return to our home in the evenings, where she took care of us all.

It may have been lucrative for white women to work outside the home, but the same cannot be said for most of the black women who took jobs in white homes. My mother earned a meagre salary as a domestic housekeeper, less than one-tenth of the average earnings of a white woman. Many white employers felt justified in paying a pittance to their black staff because they considered that the other perks they provided bolstered the cash portion: a small outside room to live in (usually without hot water and nothing more than a hole in the ground for a toilet); Thursday afternoons off; a weekend off a month; a 50 kg bag of mealie-meal and a couple of kilograms of "servant's meat" for meals. I wonder if white employers driving to the coast, or travelling to game farms for their annual holidays, ever gave any thought to the families of the women who had served them and their children for the best part of the year. We were lucky to see our mother for a full week once a year, but mostly we saw her only during the couple of hours she was able to snatch once a month.

The small salary that my mother earned could not possibly cover all our needs. Whenever she arrived home, we rushed to the packets of supplies that she dropped on the kitchen table, hoping to find a whole treasure box of goodies. Our exclamations "Omo!", "Sunlight!", "Ace Mealie Meal!", "Black Cat Peanut Butter!" may even have been heard in the next village. We fantasised about things like peanut butter, but usually we received nothing more than bare essentials such as soap powder and mealie meal. My mother's salary barely met the cost of transport between Johannesburg and Pretoria, and it was certainly was not sufficient to pay school fees – even though, at the time, school fees were only 25c per year.

My mother was a proud and hard-working woman, but faced with the prospect of her children going hungry, she did what most poorly paid domestic workers did – she helped herself to items from her employer's home, though she was careful not to be greedy. When her "madam" wasn't looking, she popped a couple of teabags into her overall pocket, a half-dozen eggs that wouldn't be missed after a month-end grocery shopping spree, and perhaps even a bar of scented soap – just the sort of thing that put a smile on our faces when she came to visit us.

Domestic workers had responsibilities, but they had no rights. My mother could not take a day's unpaid leave or an extra day at the end of a weekend; whenever we had a medical emergency, my sisters or grandparents had to help out.

"Madams in the suburbs don't want to hear stories about sick children, family funerals, weddings, or meetings with the school principal in the village," our mother would tell us when we bemoaned her long absences. Instead, she visited us on the quiet, and I think the reason for her clandestine mid-week visits was a combination of feeling deprived of time off and fear that her creative shopping expeditions in her employer's pantry might be discovered – hence her escaping into the refuge of her own home for a short while.

My mother had to time her departure from her employer's house with caution and in silence. She would wash, dry and pack away the family's dinner dishes, feed the family pet and wait until the sun slipped away. After the family had settled down for the evening to listen to the radio or read their library books, and the family pet had relieved himself of his dinner at the top end of the garden, my mother would quietly unlatch the gate at the servant's exit. Sticking to the shadows cast by the trees planted so pedantically by the parks department on the paved sidewalks, she hurried to the main road, where she caught a taxi to Park Station in Johannesburg. There she could relieve herself of her anxiety and her parcels and relax on a bench as she waited until the train to Pretoria pulled into the station. When she arrived in Pretoria, she changed platforms, boarded the train to Hammanskraal, and then travelled on to GaRamotse.

Anyone who has spent time in the African bush, isolated from electrification of any kind, will know how impenetrable the darkness can be, especially in the absence of a moon or stars. Usually, my mother arrived at GaRamotse at about ten in the evening, only to be greeted by an enveloping darkness. Weighed down by her parcels, she would trudge the sandy paths, dodging thorny bushes and ignoring scuttling animals until she reached our house.

I have a wonderful and vivid memory of one of my mother's visits when I was about five or six years old, and hadn't yet started school. I remember my mother walking through the door one evening and scooping me up into her arms and whispering my name into my ear, "Highman", and I recall being carried around by her for a long time that night.

My mother's weekend visits were especially precious occasions. After she had greeted all of us individually, she gave an indulgent smile as we inspected the supplies she had brought with her. "Yes, I managed a couple of tins of tomato this time," she said once as she stood next to my sister at the paraffin stove balanced on the kitchen table and cooked for us. During that meal and many others like it, we licked the gravy and pap from our fingers, our mouths busy with all the eating and talking, as we caught up on each other's lives.

"Has that spider bite on your arm healed yet, Highman?" my mother asked. "Come, let me have a look at it."

She held my hand towards the dim light cast by the candles and then turned to Esther and examined one of the dresses that she had altered for Conny. Holding the thin fabric in her hand, she looked up suddenly and said, "Florah, did you replace the cup of sugar you borrowed from the Parkies family?"

These were such ordinary, though precious, family moments and, like any child, I did not want them to end. I could have listened to my mother's Lexington voice for hours – though it was thick and raspy from years of smoking, it was also warm and maternal. The excitement that accompanied my mother's visits exhausted me, and though I tried as hard as I could to keep my eyes open, they would close without my being able to stop them, and gradually my mother's voice faded away as sleep overcame me.

Early the next morning, while I was still sleeping, Esther, Florah and Conny would link arms with each other and accompany our mother back to the train station. Sometimes I tagged along with them, as they all laughed and talked together about things that mostly concerned girls and women.

"Mme, don't forget Herman needs new shoes – size 6," Esther would remind her. "Try to bring some sachets for ginger beer next time; and the sugar, don't forget the sugar, or it will be terrible!" Florah would urge, pulling a face.

My sisters frantically recalled things that they had forgotten to share with my mother, jostling with one another to tell her before the 4 am train arrived and took her back to Johannesburg. After my mother left and I was unable to sense her presence any more, a post-visit hollowness would descend upon the house for a few days.

In the 1960s, several Johannesburg and East Rand suburbs were "white-by-night" zones; this meant that black people were not allowed to be on the streets during the hours of curfew that usually fell between nine in evening and five in the morning. The tree-lined streets of the suburbs were patrolled by police in vehicles that we called Black Marias. These Ford F250s were used to transport lawbreakers to police cells for curfew infringements or pass transgressions. Shouts of "Haai, wat maak julle hier!" could be heard as the heavy vehicles chased lawbreakers. Often, there was a spare tyre that rolled around in the back of the truck, which slammed into offenders as the driver took an unnecessarily sharp turn, or screamed to a sudden halt.

By 1962, the apartheid government had quelled all protests and opposition, and so all black people from the age of sixteen were compelled to carry a pass. Each individual's pass stated personal particulars, and named the geographical location in which the pass-holder was allowed to live and work. Black people were also required to carry work permits, signed by their employer or the relevant Bantu Administration officer, which were affixed to their passes. The pass and the permit were expected to be carried at all times. My mother was constantly aware that if she was caught infringing upon any of these restrictive laws, or in fact any law at all, she might be beaten or imprisoned, and might consequently lose her job. But with no alternative, no structures that allowed her to act within the law, she was forced to take the risks that hundreds of thousands of black people took daily, and to bear the possible consequences. From personal experience, I know what it was like to go to work every day in the oppressive shadow of those laws, so I can imagine how stressful it must have been for my mother who was caught between a needy family and laws that prevented her from having easy access to her children.

Despite the difficulties of life under apartheid, my mother did all she could to take care of us, and provided not only food, but also the clothing we needed as we grew bigger. New clothes were a special luxury that we did not take for granted. As a rule, we were only presented with new clothes at Christmas, and then only when we were lucky and there was money to spare. Fortunately, we were not the exception; the situation was the same for many village families. It was not uncommon for siblings to share a pair of shoes, or for boys to wear their older sisters' T-shirts; if the clothes and shoes fitted us – and sometimes even when they did not – we had no option but to wear them without complaint.

Our extended family in GaRamotse did what they could to supplement items for our family, but other families were experiencing the same economic hardships as ours, and resources could only stretch so far. In the middle of each month our food supplies would invariably run out, and in desperation we would borrow a cup of sugar or some mealie meal from a neighbour, and then at the end of the month, or when my mother sent us money, we would return the borrowed items. We lived from hand to mouth, and I could understand my brother's decision to remove himself from that environment; however, as I eventually discovered, all Pobane had succeeded in doing was swapping one dysfunctional, poor environment for an equally impoverished lifestyle. Things may even have got worse for him: by distancing himself from the strong support of family, he would certainly have felt isolated and vulnerable.

After the harsh, cold winters, life usually improved in the village. Summer's natural bounty relieved the pressure on our family's food larder. The rains came and the vines swelled; yellow, green and small black pellets plumped into juicy grapes, paw-paws weighed down the branches of the trees, and our mouths watered as we impatiently watched mango skins change from green to orange. Peaches hung from the branches of trees that we climbed during games of hide and seek.

"Be careful of spiders hiding in the branches," Florah would shout up at us, giving us away as she passed below us on her way home from school. And then, of course, there was the maize, chewy white mielies that we roasted on fires, barely able to stop ourselves from snatching them off the embers, they were so tempting. GaRamotse was reasonably self-sustaining, and growing one's own produce was satisfying, rewarding, but also absolutely necessary for many poor families.

The sunny days of summer alleviated the hardships of village life. As the days grew longer and the weather warmed, children spilled into the open spaces of the village, kicking balls, teasing dogs and smaller siblings, and running errands for older family members. Summer was also the time when practice sessions for the marching bands began, as children formed groups that performed music at social gatherings.

None of the villagers owned a radio when I was young. Prime Minister Verwoerd had declared that television was the devil itself, and it would never be allowed to entertain South Africans while he still breathed. So without radio or TV, the possibility of performing in the marching bands was an exciting one for all the youngsters in the village.

Anyone with enough enthusiasm was welcomed into the marching band. The only condition was that each participant had to make their own drum, and in the spirit of camaraderie that was a feature of village life, the younger, less-experienced drum makers were assisted by the older, more capable boys.

It was a great affair to decide what hide we'd use to make our drum – a black-and-white cowhide, or a russet brown one. Once the choice of hide was made, we carried it down to the dam, small boys like me struggling under the scratchy weight of the untreated hide. It took hours for us to wash and treat the hide, and once we'd done so, we left it out to dry for a couple of weeks. We could barely contain our excitement as we waited, and when the hide was eventually ready, we eagerly began to make our drum. We stretched the hide over a wheelbase and fastened it with cow sinew. As we worked, our fingertips were rubbed raw and bled, but the older boys usually helped those of us who could not manage the task.

At night, you would often hear the odd drumbeat. Boys in possession of their very first drums could not resist the temptation to beat them, for the pure joy of hearing the hollow sounds echo through the quiet village.

During the week, we dashed around completing our chores and getting our homework done so that we could participate in the band practice that took place every night, often in preparation for a wedding or some other village function.

"Please Esther, can't Conny fetch the water tonight, I want to get to band practice?" I pleaded, hoping to be let off my chores so that I could fully enjoy the events. At wedding ceremonies, the bride and groom were generally from neighbouring villages. Most weddings took place during December, or over the Easter holidays, as these were usually the only times when people were able to arrange time off from work.

Weddings were grand occasions; adults dressed up – men in their suits and hats and shiny shoes, women in two-piece outfits with stockings, hats and gloves. The women of the village prepared an assortment of foods that were served as a buffet. But the star of the meal was always the freshly slaughtered cow or goat or sheep – depending upon the family's financial means. As we watched the meat being cooked on the glowing coals of a fire, the fat sizzled and spat and everybody was happy if they received just a sliver of crisp skin or meat. The marching bands took great delight in leading the bridal couple through the village streets; neighbours joined in the singing and dancing until the couple reached the house where the reception was to be held.

We practised hard for our band, hoping that by Christmas we'd be good enough to be chosen to march in one of the neighbouring villages. These joyous festivities provided an opportunity for everyone in the village to participate. At night, when the practice was over, or after an event that ended in the early hours of the morning, the villagers went home. Then, across the landscape, another kind of music rang out – the deafening choir of frogs calling from the dam. Music was, and continues to be, a pleasurable and important part of my life – and that of most people who grew up as I did.

When I compare my formative years to those of Pobane, it seems to me that our lives were very similar. The only real difference was that he had grown up with a father, while I had not. Pobane had surely kicked a ball with my father, been carried on his shoulders when my father ran an errand, and had probably discussed with him details of arguments that he may have had with his friends. I had never enjoyed that father–son bond; however, if you know no different, you do not brood about things you have never experienced. I had never known my father, and unfortunately I did not have the benefit of the consistent guidance of an older brother. If Pobane had continued to live in Hammanskraal, might he have filled that parental gap for me? Perhaps urged me to hurry as we walked to the local soccer ground, or encouraged me to practise Afrikaans, even though I detested the language?

In the absence of a male figure in our home, our next-door neighbour, Mr Parkies, and my paternal grandfather offered me advice. Both men were either gentle or firm with me, depending on what I needed in each situation. My paternal grandfather favoured me over his other grandchildren – to the chagrin of my grandmother, who was fairly harsh with me and gentler with the other grandchildren. Clearly, she felt she had to make up for my grandfather's unabashed favouritism.

The village soon welcomed a new resident, someone who would introduce the wider world to the children of GaRamotse. This man would show us that the world stretched far beyond the short section of coal-line that ran between Hammanskraal and Pretoria.

Chapter 3

Poverty restricted most of the villagers to the confines of Hammanskraal, and so we had to rely on activities that we generated ourselves to provide entertainment. Whenever my mother visited, I would tug at her arm and beg her to bring a radio next time she came. The wildest dream of children in GaRamotse was for their parents to own a PM9 battery-operated radio.

Then the Baloyi family arrived. The family had been forced to migrate to our village because the government had taken over their land to establish an industrial area. James Baloyi brought with him a wind-up gramophone. We were awestruck by the music machine. The arrival of that gramophone changed the lives of the youngsters of GaRamotse. The first time we saw it we stood, wide-eyed as geckos, watching James wind up the machine, our breaths caught in our throats and our fingers plugged into our ears, unsure of what to expect.

And then the box came alive. Through the scraping needle and the scratchy speaker, the people of GaRamotse were introduced to musicians, not from our village, not even from our country, but international black musicians whose honey and gravelly voices and orchestras set our hips rolling, our knees pumping, and our minds dreaming. The songs that came out of that brown beat-up gramophone hinted to us, the children of GaRamotse, that there was a world beyond the place where our sun rose and set every day.

Singing and dancing was no longer confined to the festive season or wedding celebrations; now, on weekends, we tapped our toes to the tunes of great singers as we listened in the Baloyi's open house. We enjoyed international bands such as Diana Ross's Supremes and other Motown favourites, stars like The Temptations and Marvin Gaye, and Booker T and The MGs. We were also introduced to the music of South African musicians who were living in exile at the time, including Miriam Makeba, Hugh Masekela, Letta Mbuli, and Caiphus Semenya. Ladysmith Black Mambazo with their traditional Zulu isicathamiya, and the Mahotella Queens with their mbaqanga soon became firm favourites. The village rocked to the Motown sound that was typified by simple melodic songs where orchestras highlighted the backbeat. At these parties beer flowed, pap simmered in wobbly pots on primus stoves, thick wedges of bread were handed around, candles glimmered, and the air was hazy with cigarette and dagga smoke. These musical evenings were a refuge from the humdrum of our daily lives. In the main, life was difficult, but when we made our own fun, things did not seem so desperate.

The new soul music with its distinct pop influence mesmerised my friends and me, and my body responded to its allure; I loved dancing. Before I started smoking and drinking, I used to hang out at James's house just to enjoy the dancing. I was never a shy kid, but in that tight living room I really found my feet. I was a mover and shaker on the dance floor, and I was often the centre of attraction, with a small audience gathering around and cheering me on. New music was released every couple of months, and with each new song there was a new dance to go with it.

"Come on Highman, do the 'Hitch Hike' for us!" my friends called out whenever Marvin Gaye's hit came on, or "Hey, it's 'Where Did Our Love Go' by The Supremes!" And I would dance the "Baby Baby" during the chorus. There were also the "Camel Walk" and "The Popcorn" dances that accompanied James Brown hits of the same name.

With my spirits buoyed by my love of music, I was a cheerful person and a fairly popular kid at school. Teachers always singled me out to deliver a speech or to be the leader of a group when we had group activities; this is probably because I have always been comfortable and confident being in the limelight.

I was fortunate to have teachers who liked me and made time for me. I remember especially two primary school teachers: our neighbour, Mrs Parkies, who was my Grade 1 teacher, and Mrs Padi, from the Free State, who spoke Sesotho. Although most villagers in GaRamotse spoke Northern Sotho/Sepedi, my father's family spoke Shangaan. My paternal grandparents spoke to each other in Shangaan, but they spoke to their grandchildren in Northern Sotho/Sepedi. Although my surname is Shangaan, I still do not speak the language, even though people often expect it of me.

The days of my youth were punctuated by domestic chores, attendance at school, and a bit of fun. Everyone in our household had jobs to do, and my main responsibility was to fetch water from the village dam, as we had no plumbing. Even though I sometimes felt overwhelmed by the tasks, I soon realised the importance of everybody carrying out their duties in the home or the community to ease the burden for everyone else. But, children will be children, and when I tried to dodge my responsibilities, Esther and Florah were quick to pull me back into line. Conny and I are closest in age, and we often disagreed about trivial, childish matters. Invariably, the argument would end with her teasing me about my big front teeth: she would point at me and shout out in a derisory way, "Meno a maholo!" which means "the one with the big teeth". This kind of teasing, taunting and sibling rivalry is normal in any family, but we never had serious squabbles; generally, an atmosphere of peace and harmony prevailed in our home. This is all thanks to my parents and my older sisters, who created a calm atmosphere for me to grow up in during my parents' absence.

Florah was the least involved of my sisters: being in the middle of austere Esther and ebullient Conny, Florah kept to herself and went about her duties without too much fuss. Florah is still the beautiful, reserved woman she was when she was young. She was responsible for preparing the meals in the house, but she would not be dictated to by anyone. One morning, Conny and I were desperately hungry; it was almost noon and we hadn't had breakfast yet.

"Come, let's play on the street," Conny said, trying to distract me – we both knew what the consequences would be if we woke our moody sister Florah to demand breakfast.

"I don't want to play any more, I'm tired," I said.

It is foolish to leave two youngsters unattended, and Conny and I could contain our frustration no longer. We crept into Florah's room, knelt down at the foot of the bed, lit a piece of paper, and held it to her feet. Well, that certainly got Florah moving, but all it earned us was Florah's bad temper – we went hungry the rest of that day.

Overall, my sisters did their best to give me guidance and stability, and I have always tried to emulate their example. On the occasions that I strayed, wilfully ignoring their caution to behave, and getting myself into sticky situations, I can only blame myself for my stubbornness.

Before I was old enough to attend primary school, I was left to my own devices while my sisters attended school or work. They left the house in the early hours before I was awake, but they were always careful to leave the front door open so that when I woke up I could toddle down the path that led to the Parkies' house.

"Ah, you've woken up, Highman; come here and let me clean you up," Mrs Parkies would say in her kind voice. She would wash my face, straighten my clothes and give me a meal. Afterwards

I spent most of the day playing with the other children in the village, and we usually amused ourselves by playing soccer.

What I appreciate most about my sisters is that even though our family was fragmented, we were not a dysfunctional family. As the oldest daughter, Esther inevitably assumed the role of mother. I sometimes regret how we used to tease her about being ugly – because she certainly wasn't – but we often resented the discipline that she meted out. Esther was a no-nonsense type of person, and circumstances demanded that she be so. Even after she married Nkokoto Parkies, the young man who lived next door, she continued to play a maternal role. When my mother was away, she'd say to me, "Herman, come and stay with us; you can continue going to school and we'll look after you." She knew it was essential for me to complete my education.

When I was about eight years old, my mother's last child was born – my half-sister Nancy. I use the term half-sister, even though in black culture this is not a term that is ever used. My mother's relationship with Nancy's father is a rather vague memory, but I do recall that my mother met Nancy's father while she was working as a cleaner at a school in Bosplaas. I also remember Nancy's arrival, which my mother attributed to a helicopter delivering the baby during the night. My sister Esther's son, Silas, was born a few months after Nancy. Suddenly I was no longer the baby in the house. A few years later, Esther's second child, Nelly, was born. So I grew up with Nancy, Silas and Nelly calling me malome, or uncle.

Any village boy who was lucky enough to receive the gift of a ball was under no illusion that the ball belonged to him – it was a communal ball, kicked around on the streets of GaRamotse until it wore out, or worse, had a premature demise by landing on the sharp thorns of a nearby bush. Most often we did not have a ball, so, necessity being the mother of invention, we often used old rags to make a ball to kick around. Still, no sound was more satisfying to us village boys than the thud of a new ball bouncing on a dirt road.

The solid, stable foundation that my mother and sisters set for me was further entrenched by a deep religious faith that was embraced by the entire village. The Methodist Church was the spiritual glue that connected the GaRamotse community. It was a formal, disciplined church with an evangelical component that suited village residents; singing and dancing while giving praise was a natural way for us to show our faith in and devotion to God.

The Boloko family were especially keen supporters of the African Apostolic church, and regularly hosted vigils at the weekends, hosting celebrants in their modest home.

"Where are you off to?" Esther would ask, and I would reply, "I'm off to Gabo-Matlakala." Everyone in the community referred to the Boloko family home as Gabo-Matlakala because their eldest child was called Matlakala. The villagers often fell asleep with the sound of hymns in their ears as we eager worshippers prayed, sang, danced and drummed. We carried on like this throughout the night, and the only time we broke off was when Mrs Boloko thrust mugs of steaming tea into our hands.

"Here, drink up, your throats must be parched," she would say as she also gave us thick slices of bread.

Church provided the village children with a chance to forget our hunger and our threadbare shorts, and to yearn less for our parents; church was also a place we could enjoy ourselves.

School was far less lenient on us. Our household chores had to be completed before school started, and sometimes they took a little longer than expected. When it rained, for example, it took longer to fetch water as I trudged home along the muddy track. But school times were not negotiable. The bell rang promptly at 7.45 am every day; and the teachers had an attitude of zero-tolerance towards students who did not abide by the rules.

"You are late again, Mashaba! Make sure you present yourself at the principal's office at break time."

We did not own an alarm clock and so we woke up when our bodies felt rested, or when the chickens scratching outside our rooms indicated that it was time to get up. My first chore of the day was to hurry to the dam to collect water, then rush home to heat it so that the family could perform their ablutions. It was hit and miss whether I arrived at school on time, and there was always the vigilant teacher-on-duty, waiting with the standard stern expression of straight lips and inquiring eyebrows, ready to reprimand and punish latecomers.

Those unforgiving teachers were harsh with their punishment; they beat us and often berated us: "Too poor for school fees? Can't get up on time? It seems like a little discipline is in order to make sure you remember that school doesn't tolerate idleness."

The government may have been the oppressors at the top of the ladder, but on the lower rungs of oppression were the teachers who enforced discipline with an iron hand, and whether or not they were aware of our dire economic circumstances, they implemented every petty school rule with the same tenacity as the government that perpetrated the larger bulldog acts of oppression.

"Black shirts, black shoes; are you colour-blind, Mashaba?"

Black shorts, white shirts and black shoes were the only accepted uniform for schoolboys, and woe betide any learners who did not wear the correct uniform. School exercise books and stationery were required at the start of every school year, along with the 25c annual school fee. Collecting every cent of those fees was stressful – until we had paid our fees in full, we were either publicly ridiculed in front of our peers, or beaten by the teachers. These insensitive enforcers of rules did not distinguish between the responsibilities of parents and those of learners, and it was mostly the learners who bore the brunt of their displeasure and punishment.

When parents don't have money, they just don't have money – they're not down to their last R100 000 in the bank or withholding the payment of school fees because the money is earning a good interest rate. As a result of my own experience, I believe that free education is absolutely essential to developing countries, because without access to education, the potential of a learner is significantly curtailed; many of my peers had to drop out of primary school. It is short-sighted for governments to ignore the necessity for free education; if citizens are educated, the chances of their being self-sufficient are high, but if they are uneducated they represent a loss of talent and labour, and are a permanent drain on the economy.

When I was older and moved away from GaRamotse, I left behind friends who, because of their poverty, had to abandon their studies prematurely. I left them skulking in shebeens with little more to look forward to than their next beer. Now, thirty-five years later, whenever I return to GaRamotse, I find some of my old friends sitting on the same stools, their glazed eyes still fixated on the next beer. Many of them have never ventured out of GaRamotse to see what happens in the rest of the world – their world is confined to what little they know, they have become fearful of what they do not know, and uninterested in the world at large. Other friends who were defeated after early forays into the world complain about the unfairness of life, and unfortunately alcohol and drugs aggravate their depressed outlook on life, colouring the world in a negative shade.

The Apies River cuts through the middle of Hammanskraal. It is a swirling section of water that slaked the thirst of children in search of fun. On the occasional afternoon and during school holidays, we shuffled the five kilometres through soft sand that was like hot ash in the summer heat, dodging thorn trees and the spiny malpit weeds until we reached the shady banks of the river. Once there, we shed our clothes and threw ourselves into the water, which turned our dusty skins glossy; bright droplets clung to our hair in the sunshine.

Away from home and school, lolling on the cool riverbank in the dappled shade of the languid willows, we could just be kids. My best friend was a boy called Ntshime Ramadibane, and he and I burrowed our fingers into the muddy bank, looking for wriggly pink earthworms that we could attach to our willow-branch fishing rods. Our mouths watered at the prospect fish for dinner. Fishing is a pursuit for the patient; and while Ntshime and I sat on the muddy bank, we sang songs or teased other children splashing in the river, tossing lekgala – crabs with clicking claws – at squeamish girls, and hurling balls of clay at unsuspecting boys. In the late afternoon light, we sunned ourselves on the smooth rocks like lizards.

While certain things were beyond my control while I was growing up, there were areas where I could take control – and I did. While it was impossible for me to ensure that I had the correct uniform or the full complement of schoolbooks, and the elusive 25c for school fees, I could ensure that I did my homework each day. By having a disciplined work ethic I was able to progress well through school, and my grin-and-bear-it attitude made me a firm favourite with some of my teachers. I realised early on that a smile managed to creep into the hardest of hearts, while a grumble or a frown rewarded you with rejection. My brother's refusal to study further than Grade 8 had disappointed my family because he had achieved high marks in the final examinations, and he certainly had the intellectual capacity to pursue his studies. Because of this, my sisters and my mother wanted more for me; but I also wanted more for myself. I had grown increasingly aware of how limited opportunities were for black people, I saw how difficult it was for my brother to find and keep a job. Early on, I realised that if there was a map on which to chart my independence, part of that route could be achieved by ensuring I was properly educated.

The Grade 8 examination was an important hurdle, and Mr Ben Khase, our teacher, made sure we knew what we were up against.

"If you boys and girls want to have the life you dream of, you're going to have to work for it. Grade 8 is not for the idlers who think twice about coming to school, Grade 8 is for the learners who are willing to come to school – not five days a week, but six days a week," he said. He ignored our groans, and continued. "Yes, that means extra classes on Saturdays to boost your knowledge."

Attendance at Saturday School was never a mere option, it was expected of us, and we soon realised it was imperative that we attend those extra classes if we wanted a better future for ourselves. Mr Khase sacrificed his family leisure time to teach us, and we knew that the least we could do was reciprocate by ensuring that while our friends were going to soccer practice, we were sitting in our cramped desks listening to everything that Mr Khase had to impart. Our efforts and Mr Khase's devotion paid off, and we passed the dreaded Grade 8.

It was time to move on to high school, but leave-taking does not only comprise moving forward, it also means saying goodbye. I had been at Lebelo Primary School for eight years and I had to say farewell, not only to some wonderful teachers and friends, but also to Ntshime. I went on to Ratshepo High School in Temba township, while Ntshime attended high school in another village.

"No, we will not say goodbye for ever. I will still visit you, and you will visit me," we promised as we took leave of each other. In the months following the end of that year, we saw each other whenever the demands of high school permitted. But at the end of Grade 10 Ntshime found a job, and our friendship faded. My childhood had ended, and so had one of my most memorable friendships.

Over the years I kept in touch with Ntshime, but when I last saw him I couldn't think of a single thing we had in common to discuss, other than the usual small talk. For the past thirty years, Ntshime has worked for Waltons Stationers, and he now occupies a steady, successful sales position. But now it is difficult for us to recapture the easy way in which we related to each other all those years ago, which now seem a lifetime away.

Chapter 4

By the time I started at Ratsepo High School in Temba in 1974, I was living with Esther and her husband Nkokoto Parkies. It was a time of great political instability. The Soweto education crisis erupted in 1976, resulting in rioting and uncertainty in the townships as the police and army were mobilised to enforce stability in the townships.

"Thank God we're out of it," my mother said. For once, we were grateful that we weren't living in Soweto. Of course, we still felt that everything exciting that happened, happened in Soweto, but we were happy right then to be away from it all. For especially families living in Soweto, there was great concern for their children. While parents and guardians understood their children's frustrations with the apartheid system and the Bantu Education system in particular, they feared for their children's safety. Friends from the townships visited us in our rural area, verbalising their concern for their families.

"I'm too scared to send my kids to school. The police are on the streets, they're heavily armed. They're ready to shoot, their fingers are on the triggers," were some of the things they said.

Many families decided that the best way to protect their children was to remove them from Soweto and send them to families who lived in rural areas; in this way they could reduce their children's exposure to the dangers in the township and protect them from indiscriminate police attacks.

Louis Mkhetoni was one of those township children who

came to live in GaRamotse, and his easy-going manner and tendency to risk-taking appealed to me; in Louis I recognised aspects of myself.

Perhaps because I had grown up surrounded by adults, I seldom hung about with children my own age. Instead, I sought out adult company, and with Louis being a township boy, he seemed to me to be more street-wise, more adult than my peers. We hit it off immediately, and our friendship endures until today; he is my brother.

During my early high-school days, my mother was working at the Hepkers' home in Sandown. On her insignificant salary, she was not able to meet her family's financial demands for fees, books and food. The cost of transport was high in relation to her monthly salary, and so she could rarely afford to visit us.

"I'll try to come at the end of the month after next," she would say, her eyes holding the regret she could not afford to admit to us.

Nothing teaches survival skills better than starvation does; there were some days that we woke up not knowing if we would eat a substantial meal that day or the next. During break time at school, when most children unwrapped their lunches, I smelt their food and was barely able to control my salivating. I watched as more fortunate students raced to the tuck-shop. Often, Louis and I had nothing to eat.

"Mashaba, did you smell that pap and stew?" Louis once asked as a boy opened his lunch. A gnawing hunger ate away at us, and at break Louis raced out of the school gates and ran to the nearest house, praying that the occupants would be away at work so that he could drink from their tap. Ignoring a chained dog that protested at his trespassing, Louis positioned his mouth under the tap, then turned it on and drank deeply, as he temporarily alleviated the ache of hunger. An hour or two later in class, wedged into the desk next to me, Louis's dissatisfied stomach would complain loudly at the trickery, but his was not the only growling stomach in that wretched classroom: mine also complained – rudely and often.

When adults gathered in their small kitchens or on narrow porches, they discussed the daily happenings of their lives. Theft was common, and most adults made unashamed admissions to having stolen any manner of items from their employees.

"I can fix your exhaust pipe; I picked up a welding machine at the factory before they dismissed me," an auto repairman would say to a villager whose car exhaust dragged along the bumpy dirt road.

"What do you need – paper with or without lines? Just be patient and I'll bring it next time I'm in the stationery room at the office," a mother would reply to a child nagging for a new exercise book. A supermarket packer could often be seen walking home with a full tray of tinned food balancing on his head – tins that hadn't made it from the store room to the supermarket shelves. So many good people in the village felt the pressure of having to reconcile pressing family demands and insufficient wages. As children, we eavesdropped on the conversations of our parents and their friends, so it was an inevitable reaction that we, too, did whatever it took to ensure that our needs at home were fulfilled.

Theft in these instances was not a malicious, misanthropic or criminal act, it was an act of pure survival. We attended church on Sundays and we said our prayers with solemn faces and sincere hearts, but every week we chopped firewood that we'd stolen from a nearby farmer's land, and in the middle of the night, using only the moon to guide us, we climbed through another farmer's barbed wire fence to steal water from his dam. We usually carried out these clandestine activities in a group so that we could keep an eye out for the farmer, and when I cast my mind back to those days, I wince at the fact that we were so desperate; the game farm where we stole water was vast, and wild animals roamed about in the bush, but we were more afraid of the farmer's wrath than of being attacked by the wild animals. However, necessity often influences a person's choices. Securing water and wood went some way to satisfying our thirst and need for warmth, but it did not satisfy our hunger.

"Hey, we can't go on like this," I said to Louis one day when we were particularly hungry. Louis and I, like many other township kids, used to buy small amounts of dagga, which we smoked secretly, away from adults and teachers.

Louis looked at me quizzically. "What do you mean, my friend?"

"This is nonsense, it's getting us nowhere, just buying the stuff and smoking it, and buying more, and smoking it, day after day. What if we bought the dagga and sold it ourselves?"

We discussed this, and you could say that we decided to become dealers. Moersekont was our supplier, and his name left no room for doubt as to his being a hardened gangster. We negotiated with him to supply us with the dagga, packed it into matchboxes, and sold it for about twenty cents a box. We made a good return on our money, and we could now afford to feed ourselves from the profits we earned. It certainly wasn't an ideal way to earn a living, but resources and opportunities for two starving school kids were far and few between at the time.

Sometimes when I watch my own children today, turning their noses up at a stew that doesn't appeal or a cut of meat that does not look appetising, I remember those days. I know Connie gets mad when I complain that the children are fussy, but I cannot help recalling how absolutely empty and ill one can feel from hunger. Those memories live with me. And while I know that I cannot put an old head on young shoulders, it concerns me that it is so easy for privileged people who live in a throwaway society simply to tip a meal into a dustbin, and to make another one at a whim.

Although Hammanskraal was fairly remote, it was home to several important black institutions. In 1962, the first Deaf School for African Children was established there by Dominican nuns, and in 1967 the St Peter's Seminary for Catholic Priests was built; but a less welcome feature on our landscape was the Hammanskraal Police College. Black South African policemen were sent there for training; it was there that they learnt how to enforce their apartheid employer's laws. Because our village was so close to the training college, it was in GaRamotse that the latest set of police recruits got to sharpen their blades of tyranny. Dressed in their dark blue uniforms, with their menacing sjamboks, they patrolled Hammanskraal, their keen eyes scanning for any "suspicious" people or activities.

On many nights, we were roused from our beds by overzealous police officers banging on doors with their coshes. The neighbourhood dogs barked and howled, and we awoke, blinded by the torchlight that the police officers shone on us as they yelled, "Wake up, wake up! Where are you hiding him? We know he's here!"

It was humiliating to be at the mercy of the police, and yet we had to tolerate these invasions in silence. They carried out their raids under the pretext that they were checking to see who was sleeping in the house – looking in particular for men who should not have been there, men who were in transgression of the pass laws. The rough police officers commandeered the living room or the kitchen, their blue bulk dominating the room, their gruff voices barking out orders for the occupants of the house to present themselves and their passbooks. We despised those intrusions, but we grew used to the invasions. In fact, we felt far more threatened by the police when they confronted us on our streets.

During 1976 the police presence in the area steadily rose. The authorities realised that many Soweto kids were being sent to the rural areas, and they wanted to ensure that no new fires of discontent were ignited – they did not want another "cheeky" uprising to be sparked in the rural areas.

The police were everywhere, and my illicit business ventures were growing. In addition to dagga sales, I had embarked upon a career as a knoxman – the person in control of the dice during a gambling session. My one regret as a high school boy was that we had to go to school on Fridays. A weekend of commerce beckoned, and if I'd had Friday morning to prepare for the weekend, I'd have been able to make a lot more money, a lot earlier in the day on Saturday and Sunday. Over the weekends, I relieved many hard-working residents of extra cash that jingled in their pockets. They were given recreation and entertainment, and in return I could feed myself.

One Friday afternoon after school, Louis and I elbowed our way through the throng of learners, eager to get to our gambling den at Patel's Café so that we could buy a packet of candles and secure the dice – as the knoxman, I had to arrive early to ensure that I had a set of dice for a game.

"Come on, Louis, hurry, man. We have to go and buy the candles." We needed candles so that the gamblers would be able to see the dice when they played in the dark confines of Patel's Café. Although Pramlal Patel – the owner of the café – was not a gambler, his brother, Mosotho, was keen to throw the dice. That particular afternoon, we were carrying a stash of dagga that we had tucked into Louis's schoolbooks in case the police caught us. We were aware that a new contingent of gung-ho police recruits, eager to exercise their newly acquired skills, were out patrolling the streets. The punishment for being caught with dagga was a five-year jail term; and back in those days five years meant five years, no negotiation was entered into.

I felt tense, anxious as we hurried along. I was well-acquainted with fear. Whenever I saw a policeman, I broke out in a sweat. My mouth dried up, my armpits prickled and my body felt hot. The intimidating presence of the police in Hammanskraal continually made us feel as if we were a community of criminals waiting to be caught. I knew, too, that police officers had far-reaching rights in rural areas, and since there was no public prosecutor resident in GaRamotse, the police themselves could institute criminal proceedings.

On our way to the gambling den, a man stopped us.

"You'd better pasop, watch out for the police up there, at the bridge. They are stopping anyone who comes. And they're also searching people."

Louis and I looked at each other in alarm; we were in a predicament, but we were already approaching the bridge where the police officers were pacing in anticipation, and we had no option but to keep walking.

"Act normally; they won't even notice us, we're just school kids. Just keep cool," I said.

We rolled our shoulders and slowed our strides, adopting the typically nonchalant amble of township kids. We hoped that the school uniforms we were wearing would be to our advantage: the police would surely not expect schoolboys to be carrying passbooks. We hoped, too, that we looked younger than our sixteen years – anyone older than sixteen had to carry a passbook.

Being caught for any offence was a terrifying experience that Louis and I sought to avoid at all costs; two of our friends had been arrested for passbook offences and sent to jail for the obligatory three months. When they were released, they displayed criminal tendencies far more severe than stealing wood or putting a loaf of bread under their coats. Or selling dagga or engaging in gambling.

Louis and I were so afraid of being questioned by the police ahead of us at the bridge that we barely managed to maintain our pose. A police officer stepped in front of us.

"Ja, julle – kom hierso. Show me your passbooks," he demanded.

"No, we've just come from school, we have not got passes yet," Louis said while my eyes darted in all directions, searching for an escape route.

Without looking us, the policeman held out his hand.

"What are you carrying there – schoolbooks? Let me see them. Ja, ek ken julle, you oukies think you're too clever for the police."

Louis handed over the books to the policeman and even though I was poised to flee, I realised that we would not get very far; in any case, even if by some miracle we did manage to escape, our names would be on the books and the police would track us down. I was barely breathing as the police officer gave the schoolbooks a cursory glance and then handed them back to Louis and waved us on our way, clicking his tongue in annoyance.

"You two have got nonsense written all over your faces; but I've got my eyes on you, don't think you're too clever," he said, watching us until we were out of sight.

Although I'd felt nauseous from fear, I had managed to behave normally; I breathed out a long sigh as I said, "Eish, those boere."

"Ja, that was close," Louis said.

"Yes, too close," I said, realising I had just learnt an important lesson: the best way to avoid conflict was to mask my feelings. It was humiliating to be barked at by the police, or to be yelled at by teachers, but I had witnessed friends who had reacted emotionally to degrading situations, and their reactions, while understandable, only enraged the authority figures and exacerbated the situation for my friends. My cool attitude had kept us out of trouble.

Our dagga sales provided pocket money for food, but it was gambling that gave us extra money for entertainment. My mother had returned home due to illness, and the responsibility of providing for the entire household had fallen on my shoulders. Dagga sales did not bring in enough money to provide for all our domestic needs, and my mother had grown suspicious of the numerous visitors who came to score. So Louis and I focused our efforts on gambling.

On Friday nights, men and boys were out for a good time; the men had money in their pockets and wanted to alleviate the ache of the week's work, while the boys aimed to impress the girls. Most of the local men gathered at Patel's Café to gamble their hard-earned money in the hope that they'd win a bit more to take home to a nagging wife or an unemployed mother. Boys, on the other hand, needed whatever money they could lay their hands on to get the attention of a girl.

Impatient feet shuffled as the gamblers waited to place their bets. As the knoxman, it was my responsibility to keep law and order during the games. The punters gathered in a group around the burning candles and waited for the dice to roll. I threw the dice, and punters called out their numbers.

"One!"

"Five!"

"Come on six! Six!"

If one of the numbers was rolled, the punters who had bet on that number won, and I got a percentage of their winnings.

Playing dice is a dangerous game, particularly when you have high rollers, as there were always arguments when men lost their money. Gamblers who bet high stakes were usually armed, and I often found myself caught in the middle of grown men stabbing or attacking each other to settle an argument. The knoxman was feared and respected, and I tolerated no bad behaviour. When the big guns played, I knew it wasn't a place for young school children because I knew how volatile the situation could become, and how the game could degenerate into bloodshed over a couple of rand.

"Tšwaa, tšwaa! Out, get out! I shouted, pushing the kids out of Patel's and sending them into the darkness, even though I knew some of them needed to win a buck to stave off their hunger.

I had some lucky escapes – I could have been killed on several occasions. The gamblers were not the only danger; we often had to avoid holding a game at Patel's because of police raids. But I could not afford to lose money by giving up my position to another knoxman, so I had to be inventive.

"I've heard that the boere will be raiding us again, so let's set up a game in the bush," I said to Louis one night. He then told the usual group of gamblers where to meet.

I left the game early that evening as it was cold and I was losing money, but some of the punters tried to prolong their winning streak and were a bit too lively with their shouts. The noise alerted the ever-vigilant police, who soon descended upon them. They scattered and ran through the darkness, but Louis wasn't fast enough.

"You thought you were too clever, hey? Well, this is what you get for being too clever," the policeman yelled as he grabbed Louis by the neck. He spent three days in jail and was given sixteen lashes for gambling. I avoided sleeping at home during this time, fearful that the police might connect me to the events of that disastrous night. For days afterwards, the welts on Louis's bottom oozed blood – this was harsh punishment indeed for such a small offence. I felt very bad that he'd been caught and I'd left early, and after his release from jail I helped him to dress the wounds, ignoring his moans as I did so. To this day, Louis has the scars from this incident. Gambling was a seriously dangerous activity to be involved in – as quick money schemes usually are. Knowing what I do now, I would not have been a knoxman for any amount of money, however desperate the circumstances.

If I had been prepared to travel to Pretoria with my friends over weekends to work as a gardener in the suburbs, I could probably have earned enough money to see my family through to the end of the month. But I had no intention of allowing anyone to strip me of my dignity. Working for a white man meant having to call him Baas, and to call his son Kleinbaas – a boy who might be ten years younger than I was at the time. I had no intention of calling anyone Baas. And I had no intention of holding out my hand to a woman who said, "Kom boy, hier's jou middagete." The token meal was likely to be a stale bread-and-jam sandwich on a tin plate with a chipped mug of tea, which I would be obliged to eat at the bottom of the garden, out of sight of the white family and their guests gathered around a braai. Afterwards, while I pulled up weeds that grew between the flowerbeds and piles of dog shit, I would hear my tin plate clattering as the maid stored it under the sink in a cupboard together with cleaning detergents and pesticides. In addition to this indignity, half the pittance paid to me would have to go towards transport costs. I just could not bring myself to do this work; I would not allow myself to do it, even though there were times when I was lethargic from hunger and my friends urged me to go with them.

"Ag, come on, you'll get hot tea with three sugars if the madam is nice," they said. But I ignored the temptation, gritted my teeth, and refused.

While my friends worked as weekend labourers, I stayed home and studied or socialised, but by 5 o'clock I was at the train station to welcome them home. I laid out my dice on a smooth patch of ground next to the station platform, and all my friends rushed to greet me.

"Hey, you missed out, High Man; we had Oros today instead of tea!" one of them shouted, trying to rile me.

Once the greetings and the news and the teasing were out of the way, we got down to business. Everything they'd earned over eight hours, I won from my friends in eight minutes; it made no sense at all to sweat a whole day in a suburban garden for a few rand and a glass of Oros.

"You're lazy, man!" my friends cried when I refused to accept their offers of a job with employers who needed an extra hand during the holiday season.

Florah also joined the chorus. "Why don't you go and earn yourself some pocket money?" But I ignored all the jibes and the insults. I had another very good reason for not heading into the white suburbs – I was afraid.

Every family has its stories, and I remember sitting on my mother's lap once, wrapped in a blanket, as she and her friends chatted, listening to all the stories. When my mother's turn came, she told a story that shaped my early concept of whites. My mother settled on the rickety chair, ensuring that I was comfortable, and then she put a Lexington between her lips and lit up. She slowly inhaled, then exhaled, enveloping me in a pale grey cloud of smoke.

"Working for whites; it's not what I want for my children," my mother said. "Yes, yes, I know you get some good whites," she conceded as some other women clucked, but she wouldn't be swayed from telling her story. "My grandfather worked on a white farm, working that white man's lands from sunrise to sunset, turning the soil until his hands ached, planting until his spine couldn't straighten, and what did he get at the end of the month to show for his work? A bag of mealie meal. And then, when my grandmother had given him more children and the bag of mealie meal wasn't enough to feed them all – you know what happened then?" My mother stubbed out her cigarette and slumped in the chair.

At this point, my body tensed, just like the rest of the people listening; the room was so quiet you could have heard a snake slithering in the grass outside.

"The farmer's son wanted to show his father how good he was with his rifle; the silly boy was no higher than the tall grass on the farm, but he lifted the rifle, he held it steady, and put his eye to the sight. Then he swung the gun round, slowly, as he looked for something to shoot. The farm workers were bringing in the harvest, and there were plenty of targets for the farmer's son. Then he chose my grandfather and pulled the trigger."

The people shifted in their seats – I remember hearing this – but I didn't want to open my eyes and look at them. I was afraid at what I might see in their eyes. Hate? Despair? When I did eventually look up, I saw their slumped shoulders, their attitude of defeat. I understood why my mother did not want us to work for white people. I squeezed my eyes shut and vowed I would never put myself between the crosshairs of a white man's folly and his wrath.

Fortunately for my mother and her family, her father was a Lutheran minister. He had the opportunity and the means to move away from that hotbed of hatred, and so he packed up and went south. The family settled in Hammanskraal, where my grandfather was a preacher until the day he died.

Chapter 5

As a knoxman, I was relatively independent. I didn't have to be subservient to any white man. I made enough money to buy pap, stewing meat, bread, milk; I had enough to get to school and back every day and, most importantly, I had entertainment money. Louis and I visited shebeens where older guys hung out, and when we were not thinking up ways to relieve them of their cash, we kept our ears close to the ground, alert for any opportunities that might arise. We were hungry for a break that would earn us enough money to hit the big league. But our big break seemed elusive.

One lazy afternoon we were talking to a school friend Jankie about our situation.

"I know how you can make some big money," Jankie said.

My curiosity was piqued.

"So, are you going to tell us?" I asked.

"Some local gents have stolen a welding machine. It's from one of those new factories – in Babelegi," he said, referring to an industrial area outside Hammanskraal. "But there's a problem. The welding machine is 'hot', and those moegoes from the police college are looking everywhere for the machine. Those new boys want to make some arrests."

"OK, so what's this got to do with us?" Louis asked. I tapped him on the ankle. Jankie had seen the interest in my eyes and his confidence had taken a boost.

Louis sat back and put his arms behind his head, feigning lack of interest.

"Hey, I must decide if I fit you guys in. I know where the machine is hidden. If you two guys have got a plan for the machine, maybe there's a chance for you," Jankie said, his eyes narrowing.

At that stage I didn't have a clue as to who might be interested in buying the machine, but what I did know is that a welding machine meant a job: if you could weld, you could repair and also make things. In the townships and villages of Hammanskraal, anybody who had a welding machine could make a living repairing car exhausts, or welding gates and window frames. With this in mind, I decided that we'd get hold of the machine and worry about a buyer later; if I had possession of it, I'd have an asset in my hands.

"I've got some ideas," I pretended, trying to sound confident. "And, we'll split the money – a third for each of us."

Having no better alternative himself, Jankie agreed to my deal and we made arrangements to recover the welding machine.

We met a couple of nights later. It was moonless and dark, but Louis and I braved the bush, following behind Jankie, hoping that we would not come across any snakes. Jankie led us this way and that, along a meandering sandy path.

"Hey, Jankie, do you know where we're going or are you just guessing?" I asked as we scuttled around in the dark. I'd grown impatient, believing that we were on a wild-goose chase, but soon enough Jankie stopped.

"Here it is, here." He pointed to the ground, and I could see his eyes widen in the dark. Louis and I started digging with the shovels that we'd brought with us. We unearthed the welder, which was far heavier than I'd anticipated.

"Joh! It's so heavy," I said. "How are we going to carry it back to my house?"

My arms were already aching from all the digging, and I almost wept at the thought of having to carry the machine all the way back along the path. But, having no option, we heaved and moaned and carried it a short way, then we put it down and rubbed our hands, and then we picked it up again and carried it a little further, maintaining this stop-start method of carrying until we eventually arrived home and hid the welder in an outbuilding. But, now that the welder was in our possession, Jankie was reluctant to leave.

"So, when we sell the welder we will split the money three-ways. Okay? That's the deal, hey, High Man," he said, looking hard at me. I grabbed his hand and held it.

"A deal is a deal, Jankie. When we sell the machine, you'll get your share," I said.

The brand-new welding machine was worth about R600 – far more money than any of us had ever seen. We were so eager to earn ourselves a cut of the money that disposing of the welder become the focus of our attention. We were all excited, but I insisted that we exercise extreme caution before we offloaded it. At a shebeen one night, we found ourselves in the middle of a group of men loudly speculating as to the whereabouts of the stolen machine. I kept a straight face as I listened, knowing that the welder was too hot to move. When we left the shebeen I waited until we were well out of earshot, then I held Louis and Jankie by the wrists and swore them to secrecy.

"If you say anything about this, we're all going to go down. So shut up. If they catch us, the cops will put us in jail and throw away the key," I hissed. The thought of incarceration sobered them both up, and they promised to keep their lips clamped.

By this stage we were living in Leboneng – where, in 1977, my mother had been offered the chance of looking after a friend's house on a rent-free basis. But most people in Leboneng could not afford electricity, so Louis, Jankie and I had to rack our brains to think of someone who might want an electric welder. For days, my mind was in a spin as I tried to think of a suitable buyer, and then finally it hit me – Moersekont. He was the local kingpin, a drug dealer who lived in a village about five kilometres away, and he was the original hard-core bad guy. Everybody was afraid of Moersekont, and it was unheard of for anyone who wasn't part of his inner circle to dare approach him. But I'd had an idea, and I tried it out on Louis.

"Moersekont is our only hope," I said, knowing full well that Louis wasn't going to agree with me.

"Are you mad? Moersekont will get his guys to moer you. Those maniacs will sommer stick you," he cried, hysteria rising in his voice.

"Just listen, Louis. Moersekont's house is always lit up. He must be running all those lights from a generator. You see, if he's got a generator, maybe he needs a welder too," I said.

Louis looked at me as if I was crazy and just shook his head. So I played my trump card.

"Moersekont will make sure that our names are never given to the police. If some busybody does find out that we've sold him the welder, they won't say a word. Because it's Moersekont who bought it. Do you see now?"

Still Louis said nothing.

"Man, everyone's much more scared of Moersekont than those laaities from Police College," I said.

Louis suddenly grabbed my hand and pumped it, his eyes wild with delight as he gave a low laugh.

A few days later, Moersekont came to my mother's house to inspect the welder. I knew, though, that if my mother caught sight of him she'd be furious. I could imagine her saying, "Where are your brains, High Man? What are you doing with this thug?"

So while Louis distracted my mother, I took Moersekont to the outbuilding and showed him the welder. He grumbled a bit as he looked it over.

"I'll give you R150," he said.

"I'm sorry, the price is R300." I turned around as if to go. I knew what the machine was worth, and I could tell by the glint in his eye that Moersekont wanted it.

"Okay, I'll take it with me, and then I'll bring you the money later," he said.

I swallowed; my mouth felt dry. I struggled to seem nonchalant.

"No," I said again. "When you bring the money, you can fetch it." Though I was terrified of his lurking thugs, I managed to suppress my fear.

"Right. I'll come back this afternoon with the money." Then he turned on his heel and left.

Although Louis and I laughed about my bravado, I realised the power of being neutral and showing no emotion, especially when it came to negotiating. It is a lesson that was born out of fear and intimidation, and it proved invaluable in developing negotiating skills that I later used in all my business dealings. Johan Kriel, one of my first business partners, used to say that he did not know where my ability to sit out tense negotiations came from – well, this ability had its roots in situations like the one involving Moersekont.

True to his word, he arrived that afternoon and paid us the R300. Louis and I were dizzy with delight. We had never had that much money in our lives; we took the wad of notes to my bedroom, closed the door, lay on the bed, threw the blue R2 notes into the air, and laughed as they rained over us; the feeling of having so much money was euphoric. The following day we met Jankie and gave him his share – R100.

"Who did you sell it to?" Jankie asked, seeming to waver between taking the money and asking for more, hoping to negotiate a bigger share for himself.

"To Moersekont," I said.

Jankie swallowed and grabbed the money. I knew then for sure he'd never be persuaded to turn on us if pressurised by his friends or the police.

That was our first big windfall, and I admit that my fingers itched to blow the money in a big way.

"I know what I'm going to spend my money on," I said to Louis.

"What?" he asked.

"A car. A black-and-white Mini that's for sale. I'm going to buy it. Hey, imagine how impressed the girls will be," I said.

I wanted that Mini badly; for months, I had fantasised about owning a car, and impressing the girls.

Fortunately, Louis tempered my ambitions. "Are you mad? Us two boys arriving at school in a car? What do you think they'll say?"

"Ja. They'll say we were up to nonsense," I said, and we both burst into laughter.

I realised the recklessness of my desire, and agreed that buying a car would draw unwanted attention to us.

"Okay, then, let's go to Babelegi and buy ourselves some All Star shoes, Dobshire trousers, and London Fog fedoras," I suggested. Louis sighed with relief that common sense had prevailed, and off we went.

The following weekend, we hit the shebeens, each with a girl on either arm; we partied non-stop – dancing, drinking and throwing money around.

When life is hard, you quickly realise that you have to be resourceful or die. I was tired of walking to school in shoes with flapping soles, tired of Louis having to rely on an unattended tap to fill his stomach. I was no longer prepared to submit to poverty, so gambling, dagga peddling and petty crime laid the foundation of my initiation into entrepreneurship.

I was extremely lucky that I never became addicted to drugs or alcohol. When we didn't have enough money for a loaf of bread or a packet of mealie meal, we bought 20c bottles of benzene that were generally used to remove dirty marks from laundry. But I didn't use the benzene for laundry; I sniffed it. I placed a cloth over the lid and inhaled the vapour, and within seconds I was completely out of my mind. When I was high on benzene I was able to shut out everything – I could have walked through a field of thorns and I would not have felt a thing. I also tried smoking cigarettes, but because this brought on severe coughing bouts, I was forced to stop.

While I share fellow motorists' annoyance when stopped at traffic lights by glue-sniffing kids begging for money, I understand why these children hang out on street corners, sucking at plastic bottles. I've experienced that same sense of wretchedness. I am thankful for the invisible hand of God that steered me away from addiction and a wasted life. Pobane was not so lucky, however. He had developed a taste for alcohol, and it gripped him so tightly that he was never able to release himself from its hold. It was alcohol that ended up killing him. On the day that he had the fatal accident in 1988, he had been out drinking with his colleagues.

Looking back on my boyhood, I admit that I am not proud of some of the things that I have done. But because I was not prepared to work for whites in the suburbs, I had to work for myself – and that meant taking advantage of the meagre resources that were available in the township. And most of the time, my choices were not legal.

Chapter 6

I developed a strong sense of black consciousness while I was growing up. Of course, Black Consciousness as an ideology has a long history, and I had no idea at the time of its origins or development. It was only later that I learnt about the advocates of Black Consciousness and their popularisation of the "Back to Africa" idea, with its call for an end to colonial rule, and its plea for the decolonisation of black people's minds – ideas that filtered down to South Africa during the 1950s with Robert Sobukwe and the Pan Africanist Congress.

I was not consciously aware of any of this history, but as a young black male growing up under apartheid, I inevitably developed a sense of black consciousness; how could I not? Our families and friends were bringing home horror stories on a daily basis, accounts of exploitation by whites, random demeaning acts of violence towards black people – the stories never ended. Newspaper posters continually headlined the saga of racism. One story featured employers who were arrested for allowing the children of their domestic workers to spend the Christmas holidays in the suburbs with their mothers; another reported on black nurses in Ladysmith who were only permitted to attend to white patients when the patients were asleep or anaesthetised; yet another concerned black members of a Methodist church in Amanzimtoti who were prevented from attending services because a white neighbour objected to the congregants passing by his front gate.

As teenagers in the mid-1970s, my friends and I traded such stories as we sat smoking and drinking in the shebeens; we joked that one day when blacks took over the country we would make whites suffer for their crude and cruel racism.

"A pass! I won't make them carry passes, I'll make them wear big signs around their necks: everyone will know their age, their marital status – and it will give their criminal offences," one man said.

"Yes, the sign must be so heavy they can barely walk," his neighbour laughed.

"Anyone who does not wear the sign will be arrested," we all agreed.

Although we joked about acts of retribution against racists, it was our way of defusing the anger and humiliation we felt.

There were laws that governed every aspect of our lives. The Group Areas Act (1950) decided where we could live, usually in villages or towns far from any employment. Two years later, the Natives (Abolition of Passes and Co-ordination of Documents) Act – commonly known as the Pass Laws – entrenched the Group Areas Act, defining the areas where we could work. These areas were dumping grounds, or otherwise dormitory townships, for workers in the cities some distance away. The 1949 Prohibition of Mixed Marriages Act was amended in 1957 to forbid all sexual relationships across the colour line. A year later, the government passed the Riotous Assemblies Act, which allowed the Minister of Justice to stop political gatherings, specifically those of the South African Communist Party (SACP). However, from the 1960s, the government prohibited public meetings of Black Consciousness groups such as the Pan Africanist Congress and other banned political organisations such as the African National Congress and the SACP, forcing these groups to hold their meetings in secret. In Hammanskraal, people often whispered behind their hands about planned local political meetings.

"There's a meeting at St Peter's this weekend; pass on the word."

The St Peter's Seminary in Hammanskraal hosted many Black Consciousness meetings where national leaders from various religious, black and left-wing political organisations congregated to voice their displeasure with apartheid structures. These groups believed that if their dissatisfaction was registered in a collective voice, they might influence the restrictive racial policies of the time.

Hammanskraal was at the time one of seven regions that fell within the borders of Bophuthatswana, a "homeland" that the South African government had set up in 1961 for the Tswana people (the "homeland" was later given "self-rule" in 1971, and finally "independence" in 1977). We were never fooled, though, by the government's attempted deception regarding self-governance, the protection of Tswana culture and the accelerated industrialisation of the area.

It was all part of the grand scheme of apartheid, and we knew it. "This is rubbish. Afrikaners are only interested in protecting their own culture," people said. The Black Consciousness Movement saw these Bantustans for what they were – a separation of black people which should not be tolerated; it was a clear divide-and-rule strategy.

Most people in Hammanskraal were opposed to the proposed "independence" of Bophuthatswana. To protest against the government's plan, the Black People's Convention (BPC) held a meeting at St Peter's Seminary in Hammanskraal on 25 July 1977. The BPC had been established five years before by various black groups in South Africa; it excluded whites, and propagated the notion of black communalism. Arising out of the matters discussed at this meeting, the BPC wrote an open letter to Chief Lucas Mangope – the President-in-waiting of Bophuthatswana – protesting against the independence of the so-called homeland. This perceived act of defiance had people talking, and it had angered the government. Those of us who were living in Hammanskraal at the time read newspapers that had published summaries of the letter, and we gathered on neighbours' porches to listen to radio stations that aired snippets of the letter. *The World* newspaper, which most of us read, published the letter in its entirety.

Black organisations mobilised against the government's Bantustan policy, and the Azanian People's Organisation (AZAPO) visited the chiefs that represented several of the affected areas in order to drum up support against the balkanisation of the homelands. While some chiefs wanted to record their resistance to the establishment of homelands, others were too afraid to protest because they feared brutal reprisals from the South African government. However, in spite of the protests, on 1 May 1971 Lucas Mangope was sworn in as Chief Minister of the Bophuthatswana Legislative Assembly, and he retained this position in the first Bophuthatswana elections that were held on 4 October 1972.

Instead of the promised separate development and self-governance that the South African government assured the homelands they would enjoy, the newly appointed Bophuthatswana government began to sell land in areas such as Babelegi. Until this area was proclaimed in 1969, black residents from Hammanskraal had used this land to graze their cattle.

My grandfather owned a sizeable herd of cattle, and he was one of those who had farmed in the area. While he had no legal tenure to the land, he had grazed his cattle there for many decades. Gradually, however, he was forced to sell off his herd, and he returned to live in the village.

"You're not farming any more?" his friends asked.

My grandfather's eyes flashed with anger as he said, "These government people, hey, they did not notify us of their intention; they did not consult any of the chiefs or anyone else; these new Bophuthatswana government officials have divided Babelegi into small industrial plots, and they have rented them and even sold some to whites who want to put up factories." He shook his head. "These whites have forced us off the land. We had to sell off our animals or find other grazing areas."

But not everyone was as miserable as my grandfather. It is human nature to be optimistic when change takes place, and initially there was excitement among many villagers in the greater Hammanskraal area. They were hopeful that Bophuthatswana would mean a positive change in their lives.

"My father is leaving his job at the mine in Carletonville. He is going to get a factory job in Babelegi."

"Yes, my aunt left her job as a domestic in Johannesburg. She is also going to work in the factory in Babelegi."

These were the common threads of conversation among people in Bophuthatswana – locals who were hopeful that the establishment of Babelegi would mean that they too could enjoy the companionship of friends and family who would now have the opportunity of working close to home. Local residents were indeed employed in Babelegi businesses and factories, but black participation was allowed only insofar as it complemented white participation; blacks had jobs as lowly paid labourers, while management jobs were still reserved for whites.

I listened to the chatter, the hopes, and the optimism, but it frustrated me that people living in the homelands considered themselves to be free.

"We're not free," I said to Louis and my friends, "all we have done is swop one restrictive government for another one."

Many people soon came to realise that the unilateral actions of the Bophuthatswana government merely reflected those of the discriminatory South African government. This kind of hoodwinking and repression fuelled my growing awareness of Black Consciousness, and I was determined not to succumb to white oppression – or, for that matter, oppression by anyone. I had endured an empty belly for many years as a child, and now that I was older, I could certainly stave off further pain and humiliation by avoiding interaction with people who sought to make me a stranger in my own country, South Africa. I decided that I would define myself, that I would not be defined by anyone else's notion of what or who I should be. I would embrace a way of life in which I would not have to compromise myself or the future I wanted for myself.

After 1974, with Percy Qoboza as editor, *The World* newspaper provided a view of South Africa that described the situation as most blacks experienced it. I suppose you might say that *The World* thumbed its nose at the government and, in doing so, it reflected the experiences of most black people.

The effects of the Babelegi factory set-up were felt throughout the surrounding communities, and these effects were far from positive. In 1978, when I was a Grade 11 pupil, a local incident caused a stir in the community. Like many other factories, Saint John Knitware did little to improve the lot of local people. It traded as Sweater Girl and employed local residents, but the R3 weekly wage that employees were paid was barely enough to live on.

"How are we supposed to feed our families?" the workers complained. "It's nothing more than exploitation."

News of the workers' dissatisfaction reached mainstream newspapers, which sent their journalists to investigate the story. The newshounds tramped the streets of Babelegi and Hammanskraal, urging locals to introduce them to workers who were prepared to talk, but instead of being receptive to the journalists and welcoming their coverage of the story, the workers hid in doorways and crouched low in shebeens.

"How can we talk to the press? If we talk about the things that are happening at the factory, we're going to lose our jobs. We need the salaries, even though they are so low." The workers simply did not have the luxury of courage.

I remember watching as a group of journalists walked away, dispirited. My friend, Gilly Sebotsane, who worked for Sweater Girl, stamped his foot in frustration.

"I know I am hiding the truth," he said, "but I can't afford to lose even that insulting wage."

"So what can you do? Or what can I do?" I asked. I was equally frustrated at the predicament the workers were in and I really wanted to do something to help.

"Are you serious about helping?" Gilly asked, and I nodded.

"Okay, then. Maybe you can take proof of the exploitation to the newspapers?"

"Yes, I told you. I'll go to Joburg and give some workers' payslips to *The World*," I said.

Gilly gave me the payslips and I caught the train to Johannesburg that afternoon. I knew that the government did not like Percy Qoboza's newspaper, but I was prepared to risk having the payslips in my possession. That train journey to Johannesburg seemed to take hours, and I imagined everybody's eyes burning through my clothes into the pocket that held the payslips. Every time the carriage doors clicked open I felt certain that members of the Special Branch would descend upon me, seize the payslips, and put me in a cell from which I would never emerge.

When I finally arrived in Johannesburg, I avoided eye contact with every policeman I passed on the streets, certain that if they looked at me they would be able to read the guilt on my face. I could barely swallow, my throat was so dry.

When I reached the offices of *The World*, I explained that I had information about the situation of workers in Babelegi. The receptionist told me to wait and made a call. Soon afterwards, I was shaking hands with Thami Mazwai, the journalist covering the story at the time. I felt a huge wave of relief as I told him my story.

"I have the proof you need about Sweater Girl in Babelegi exploiting workers," I said, ignoring the tremble that travelled from my hands to my voice as I handed over the payslips.

Thami Mazwai leafed through the payslips.

"This is exactly what we need to run the story – thank you, it is incontrovertible evidence," he said, smiling.

It was a small triumph for the workers at the Sweater Girl factory and I felt pleased and proud that I'd been able to assist them. On the return journey, I savoured my first sweet pleasure of having done something that contributed to justice; it left me feeling far, far better than when I'd received the R300 from Moersekont. I felt liberated. There were many times when we felt frustrated at our inability to stand up against indignities suffered by our people, but there were not many opportunities where we could stand up and actually make a difference; for me, though, this was one such opportunity.

In 1977, a few months after the BPC had met at Hammanskraal, Steve Biko died in police detention. The response to his death was one of fury.

"There are twenty thousand people at Biko's funeral, King William's Town is full of BC supporters," my mother told me, her ear glued to the radio. But many buses and cars carrying mourners were turned away at police and army roadblocks set up around the country. The government did not allow people to grieve, and instead the police detained many Black Consciousness activists. In addition, eighteen organisations and three publications were banned, including *The World*; Percy Qoboza was arrested and later jailed. Soon afterwards, the newspaper was closed down.

There was no getting away from the effects of the government crackdown, which had an impact on all of us in some way or another. It was in the midst of this political tumult that I had to prepare for my final school exams.

Chapter 7

The sun-bleached landscape of Hammanskraal was the backdrop to our lives, but it was nevertheless full of opportunities for entrepreneurs with ideas. When you are poor and you do not have resources at your disposal, you learn to be creative with whatever opportunities or resources are available. Necessity is very often the mother of invention, and we did our best to get on top of our dire circumstances.

By the time Louis and I had reached matric, we were living quite well in Leboneng, where we had both moved to in 1977. We still had occasional clients stopping by at the house to buy dagga, and we sometimes brought girlfriends home. In the townships, young men were graded by their peers according to the number of girlfriends they had – the more girlfriends you had, the higher status you were perceived to hold by the community. The money I earned from gambling continued to provide for our weekly household expenses and I still had enough for Louis and me to live on. My mother turned a blind eye to all this – and though I was aware that she did not approve of my lifestyle, I nevertheless continued in this way.

During exam time Louis and I worked hard.

"Come and study with us; we've started a study group at our house," we said to our schoolmates.

"What's the catch?" the sceptical girls asked.

"We provide the place, and the rest of you can bring something to eat and drink." I replied with a smile. The girls seemed relieved that for once our ulterior motives appeared to be no more sinister than study and snacking.

At the study meetings we paired off and studied subjects we had in common; we worked late into the night, and sometimes into the early hours of the morning.

Our teachers were eager for us to pass, and in support of our efforts, they provided us with past matric papers. Louis and I spent long hours working through these papers, researching and answering the questions. Once we had prepared a memorandum of answers, we invited other students to the house and then we spent afternoons discussing both the questions and the answers; by the time everyone went home, most of us felt satisfied that we had a clearer understanding of the work.

"You guys have helped us a lot," they'd say, but what I discovered is that I was the one who had benefited greatly. It really is true that the best way to learn is to teach.

One day, Louis arrived at home, literally rubbing his hands with glee.

"Hey, man! I hear that the Agriculture paper has been leaked – you can get it on the black market in Atteridgeville," he said. After a brief debate, he decided to see if he could buy the exam paper. The crafty vendor who claimed to have the exam paper was taking money from desperate students with the promise that it would be available for collection a couple of days later. But something warned Louis that things were not quite right, so instead of handing over money for the paper, he called the vendor aside.

"Look, here's my address, come to the house when you've got the paper and then we will pay you for it," Louis said. The other buyers queuing behind Louis were impressed by his savvy, and they too wrote down their addresses for delivery of the exam paper. Days passed, but no word was received from the vendor.

The following week, during the mid-morning school break, Louis broke into a sweat.

"Don't look now, but the police are here. They're over there, with that guy from Atteridgeville, the one I tried to buy the Agriculture paper from," he said.

I could hear the panic in his voice, and told him, "Just relax. We didn't do anything wrong." I quietly reassured him, "We haven't got the paper; we received nothing from him. Just because the police have our address, does not mean that they can prove anything."

When break was over, the headmaster called Louis and me to his office. By the time we had tucked our shirts into our trousers and straightened our ties, Louis had calmed down; we felt confident that we could handle the policemen and manage an interrogation from the Education Department officials.

"I think you boys will recognise this address," one of the officials said as he held out a piece of paper with our address written on it.

"Yes, it's where we live," said Louis. "I went to a house in Atteridgeville because I wanted to buy the exam paper. But I only left our address and told the guy to contact me when he had the paper. I didn't buy anything; I haven't done anything wrong."

Though his admission frustrated the officials, they could not prove that Louis had acted illegally. But they decided to give him a fright anyway – scare tactics were regularly employed by the police.

"Ja, Mkhethoni, you think you're so smart. Well, you can present yourself to Pretoria Central Prison next Saturday and see if the people there find your story convincing," the investigating officer said.

The brutality of the guards towards prisoners at Pretoria Central was legendary and I was afraid for Louis. I organised a prayer group, and on the Friday night our friends and fellow students came to our small house in Temba and we held a vigil, praying throughout the night for Louis, hoping that he would not be charged with some obscure new law that could keep him in jail for an indefinite period. Early the following morning we walked Louis to the train station, patting him on the back and offering words of encouragement, but I admit that my heart was hammering for my best friend.

When Louis arrived at the old red-brick prison building, he was signed in at the double wooden gate and led to an interrogation room. The streetwise Louis immediately felt certain that he was being observed and decided that his interests would best be served if he kept his cool. When the policemen sent the other "accused", the vendor from Atteridgeville, into the room, Louis ignored him, pretending that he had never met him before; he also ignored the fellow's feeble attempts at conversation. If anyone was watching, they'd be persuaded that Louis had had no previous dealings with the other accused. The authorities apparently decided that the blood-spattered walls and menacing sounds of the prison had given Louis enough of a fright, so they summoned him, saying, "You can go, Mkhethoni, but now we know what a skelm you are, so you'd better know we're watching you, hey." They allowed him to leave.

Of course, because of all the leaks that year, the Education Department ensured that new examination papers were issued, but fortunately Louis and I had studied hard with the aid of past papers. We both passed well, with the exception of Afrikaans, which had never been my strong subject. Since the Soweto Riots in June 1976, there was a general hatred of the Afrikaans language among us because we considered it to be the language of the oppressor. The only time I opened my Afrikaans books was during Afrikaans lessons; I made no effort to master the language; I hated not only the language, but also the Afrikaners who spoke it. This was a short-sighted decision that would have a negative effect on my university experience; but it was a decision that would be revisited, and reversed, later on in my life.

The truth about dreams is that some people get to live their dreams and others do not. Louis and I had great plans for the future, but unfortunately Louis could not afford to go to university. Pobane thought that his future lay outside the mainstream, and so he abandoned education, but it was my abiding dream to go to university. Aware of our weak financial situation, I nevertheless confided in my family, telling them my feelings regarding the importance of education.

"I know that we have very little money, that we barely survive; but I really believe that a university education is the only way I can escape this life-sentence of poverty," I said.

My family all nodded in agreement, and we discussed the situation fully, making plans as to how this might be done. From then on, they all pulled together to ensure that I would realise my dream. They were aware, of course, that this would benefit them too.

In the late 1970s my mother gave up domestic work and got a job nearer home, at St Peter's Seminary. She worked hard in her job as a general cleaner, and was devoted to the church. Soon afterwards, she insisted that I convert to Catholicism.

"I hate those catechism classes," I complained to my mother as she watched me prepare for my walk to the Seminary one afternoon. I dreaded the long hours in a classroom, listening to a priest explaining the tenets of Catholicism in preparation for my first Holy Communion.

"Yes, well, you can hate them, but you must go," she said.

My mother's insistence paid off. When it came to securing a bursary to attend the University of the North, St Peter's Seminary came to my aid, agreeing to pay half the annual fees.

"So, Herman, how bad were those catechism lessons?" My mother asked with a twinkle in her eye.

Barclays Bank granted me a student loan for the balance of the fees, and Esther and her husband, Nkokoto, agreed to stand surety for the student loan.

I was admitted at the University of the North – also known as Turfloop – in 1979. I was an idealistic youth, and I was set on studying law, as I hoped I'd be able to embark upon a career that would make a difference in the world. Unfortunately, during the first week of orientation at the university, my hopes were completely destroyed. I was refused admission to study towards a BJuris degree because of my poor Afrikaans matric mark – I tasted the bitter fruit of my refusal to persevere with the hated language while at school.

As a result, I enrolled for a BAdmin degree, majoring in political science and public administration. I had absolutely no intention of ever working for the apartheid government, so I set my sights on becoming an academic. I committed myself to graduating as a political scientist, hoping that one day I would be able to leave the country and become a lecturer at a university outside of South Africa.

The University of the North was originally conceived in 1956 by fourteen traditional leaders from the northern and western regions of the country who met under a wild fig tree in the veld. Their plan was to petition the government to build an agricultural college that would serve the sons of traditional leaders. These black leaders hoped to encourage development in the impoverished rural areas, but the government was quick to realise that the idea supported its policy of separate development. As it turned out, the agricultural college was never built, and instead the University College of the North was established in 1959. Initially it was named Turfloop, which was the name of the farm it was built on, near Polokwane. In 1970 it was renamed the University of the North (Unin), and in 2005 Unin merged with the medical university of Medunsa, when its name was changed to the University of Limpopo.

Turfloop was under-resourced under the apartheid government, and it was derogatorily referred to as a bush college, or a tribal college; it had the reputation of being a second-class university. The government modelled many of the buildings on the traditional malapa, and so lecture halls were built with a semi-circular seating arrangement, which reflected that of traditional tribal meetings. At best, the students regarded this gesture as patronising. Turfloop was at the time under the aegis of the University of South Africa (Unisa). In 1961 the first Student Representative Council (SRC) was elected at Turfloop, which allowed students to voice their opinions and exercise their rights. They protested against the poor quality of the food and eventually resorted to throwing their food on the floor and against the walls. Whenever they tried to protest or consult with the rector at his residence, they were kept at bay by the rector's vicious dogs, and refused entry.

In 1968 the South Africa Students' Organisation (Saso) was established to protect the interests of black students. In July of the following year, it was inaugurated at Turfloop; Steve Biko, a former medical student at the University of Natal, was appointed president of the national organisation. When Unisa's academic trusteeship of Turfloop came to an end in 1970, students protested because they feared a lowering of standards. These were turbulent times, and they came to a head in 1972 when Onkgopotse Abram Tiro, a Saso leader at Turfloop, was expelled for a speech that he made at a graduation ceremony. White staff members were able to attend the graduation ceremonies, while black parents were forced to stand outside and watch from an open door or window. Tiro criticised the Bantu Education system, which taught black people to become slaves. He prophesied that at some future date all South Africans would be free, and that nothing, not even the powerful South African Defence Force (SADF), would be able to stop that. Tiro refused to apologise for his speech, which became known as the "Turfloop Testimony". His expulsion was endorsed by the University's Council, and both the SRC and Saso were suspended.

The Tiro incident was an expression of a wider political

activism aimed at destroying white domination. In 1977 the university council appointed its first black rector, Professor WM Kgware, believing that a black rector would restore peace to the campus and promote a general feeling of solidarity among black staff and students. But this didn't happen, as many students saw Kgware as a mouthpiece of the apartheid government, a sell-out.

These were exciting times, and I was glad I'd exchanged village life for the Unin campus. As a full-time student, I could no longer live in Hammanskraal, as we were expected to live on campus. Entering university was a defining stage in my life; I was embracing adulthood and leaving the waywardness of youth behind me. I accepted that I could no longer sell drugs or set up a gambling school on campus, and that I'd have to find other ways of surviving. It took some getting used to, not having the luxuries I'd become so accustomed to when the money was flowing freely. I often had to spend my last few coins on a desperate phone call to my sister, Conny.

"Please, sisi, can you send me a couple of rand to see me through to the end of the month?" I'd ask, and she always obliged, but my life certainly was nothing like as comfortable as it had been during my last few years at high school. Sometimes, it felt as though the easier route would have been to give up my studies and start working, but I knew an education was imperative if I was to move up through life. If I did not discipline myself and make the best of my opportunities at Turfloop, there was no way I'd be able to live my life on my own terms.

Like all bush universities, Turfloop was for black students only, and while there were a few black academic staff members, they usually held junior positions; the majority of senior academic staff members were white. I often wondered if there was a special college that bred some of the disagreeable lecturers who taught us. There was one particularly unpleasant lecturer, a Mrs Cloete, who taught us practical English with a heavy Afrikaans accent.

Unkind and abrasive, Mrs Cloete took it upon herself daily to remind us all that we were useless losers.

"You boys and girls are wasting your time; you'll never get anywhere," she kept reminding us.

There was another particularly unkind Afrikaans-speaking lecturer, Professor Swanepoel, who haunts my memories. He had been seconded from the army to teach us Economics. The 1976 Soweto riots were fresh in our memories, and many townships were still patrolled by uniformed soldiers and policemen. Inevitably, Swanepoel's army uniform did not engender among us any amiable feelings. I still wonder whether he dressed in that uniform on purpose, to intimidate us, or if he was simply too lazy to change between shifts, or whether he was compelled to wear the army uniform. Whatever the case, Swanepoel was an uncharitable man, and he failed to enrich our lives in any way at all.

As the end of the first academic year approached, I realised that I was not going to pass Economics – our lecturer had certainly made no attempt to assist his students. I knew that if I hoped to proceed to the second year I needed to pass Economics, but I decided that if I focused exclusively on that subject, I would perform poorly in all the others. To avoid failing outright, I concentrated on the subjects I knew I could pass. When it came to the end of the year I had to repeat Economics, but I was permitted in any case to proceed to the second year. St Peter's Seminary and Barclays Bank were satisfied that I was progressing satisfactorily, and they agreed to extend their assistance. With my fees taken care of, I was admitted into the second year of study in 1980.

Chapter 8

University life suited me; I enjoyed the stimulation of the studies, the intellectual interaction with my peers, and the social contact. I had made good friends at university and usually spent weekends with them as it was too far to travel home every weekend. But still, the long vacations were the highlight of university life, and I looked forward to the leisure time that I would spend with family and friends at home.

Occasionally, I would meet up with Louis in Soweto, or he would come to Pretoria and we would go on a shebeen crawl, meeting girls and partying. It was 1979, and the word "marriage" did not yet feature in my vocabulary – I relished my bachelor status and had no intention of settling down with wife and children until I was in my late thirties. My friends and I considered ourselves to be party animals, believing that we could play the field for as long as we liked. As before, the respect we got from our peers was directly related to the number of girlfriends we had, and so we earned ourselves the trendy nickname "The Ivys" – after an American R&B group who lived the high life and wore trendy clothing like bellbottom trousers and platform shoes – though these fashions reached South Africa only sometime later.

In 1978, during my matric year, I had attended a beauty pageant held at Hans Kekana High School, a popular boarding school in Hammanskraal named after a local chief in the area. I decided with Louis and two other friends, Selby and Ntja, to go fishing for girls at the pageant. But we needed bait. A car was always a definite lure for females, and we wanted to arrive at the pageant in style. Ntja's uncle was a pastor at a local church and he owned a kombi; so on the day of the pageant I cornered Ntja.

"We'd like to 'borrow' your uncle's kombi for the night," I said.

"Sorry, I can't do it; I have to drive the church choir to an engagement," he said.

Louis and I worked in tandem to ensure that our only chance of a ride was not scuppered. "What about that girl that you liked?" Louis said to Ntja.

"Yes, she'll be there, Ntja. You think a pretty girl like that will just sit around at home, staring at the wall?" I added. "If you want to see her, you'd better make a plan." I gave Louis a sideways smile.

The promise of the girl being at the pageant was all the encouragement Ntja needed, and so he faked engine trouble, thus ensuring that his uncle wouldn't be using the kombi that night.

We arrived at the pageant in the kombi and the event was already in full swing. When we got to the door, the organisers stepped in front of us.

"Sorry, no latecomers," they said, and we had to stand outside, peeping into the hall through a crack in the door. My practised eye soon spotted a girl wearing a bathing suit and a red cape, with dainty white shoes. She was the most beautiful woman I had ever seen. Minutes later, I heard the master of ceremonies say, "And the 1978 winner of Miss Hans Kekana High School pageant is Connie Maloka." My judgement had been validated, and I smiled broadly to myself.

After the crowning ceremony, I went up to Connie and introduced myself, hoping that the charm I used successfully on so many other girls would impress her. She was friendly, but she had an air of detachment.

"I'm pleased to meet you, but I already have a boyfriend," she said. I shrugged off this gentle rebuke and went with Louis to a shebeen, where we met up with some other girls who were more receptive to our flirting.

The next year, while I was at home during a university break, my cousin Shirley Sebopa and I were messing around. "Remember the girl who won the beauty pageant, the one that you liked – Connie – well, I heard that she has broken up with her boyfriend," Shirley told me.

"Oh, you have to arrange a meeting with her," I replied.

Connie was nothing like the other girls I knew; she was quiet and composed, but she was also lots of fun. The prospect of marriage hadn't entered my head, but as we got to know each other better, I knew that she'd be the girl I would marry. In actual fact, Connie had not broken up with her boyfriend, but she did tell me that she liked my ambition and drive. It would be a few more months before she eventually decided to end her relationship with her boyfriend.

My mother had silently tolerated the girls I had brought home to our house in Hammanskraal, but when I met Connie, I knew she'd be someone my mother would approve of. I did not want my mother to be under the impression that Connie was just another one of the loose girls I hung around with. So, when the next university break approached, I sat at my desk in my dorm room at Turfloop and wrote a letter to my mother:

"Dear Mum, I would like to introduce you to a girlfriend of mine. May I bring her home for the weekend in two weeks' time?"

Though my sisters and mother were surprised at my formality, they took my letter seriously, and this pleased me. My mother did not send me a reply, but she warmly welcomed Connie and me when we arrived at the family home in Hammanskraal.

From the moment I introduced Connie to my mother they liked each other, and their mutual fondness for each other pleased me; they enjoyed a close and affectionate relationship until my mother died in 1996. My mother treated Connie with the same tenderness reserved for my sisters. My sisters, too, were enamoured with softly spoken Connie. Introducing my future wife to my family in this formal way was appropriate; it let everyone know that I respected Connie and considered our relationship to be a serious one.

Connie and I kept in touch by writing to each other regularly. I would regularly receive a "Darling Herman" letter at university, and immediately after I'd finished my studying or preparation, I wrote her a "Darling Connie" letter, which I posted the next morning. Through these letters we came to know each other. However, at the weekends that I did not return home, I was not exactly faithful to Connie. As far as I was concerned, until I had a ring on my finger I was still single, and I was not going to hide in the dorm on my own when there was so much fun to be had.

Finances were tight for just about every student, and the only way to lure girls to our hostel room was to pretend that we were hosting a big party in our dorm.

"Are you coming to the party on Friday night? No? What a pity, everyone will be there," I lied.

Of course, we only invited a couple of girls because our aims were not exactly principled. We could only afford to buy cheap box wine, and so we agreed that we'd get the girls drunk so that they'd hopefully be more receptive to our less than honourable intentions. My friends and I pretended to drink, but in fact we just shared a glass of wine, or we made one glass last all night. It was a tricky situation, ensuring that none of us guys drank too much of the one precious box of wine. Our plan invariably worked. It was a mean trick that exploited the girls, but it worked for us guys.

During the time I spent in Hammanskraal, I was a devoted boyfriend, believing that Connie was none the wiser about my infidelity.

Eventually, she decided I should meet her family. But my introduction to Connie's family was quite different from her formal introduction to my mother.

"When are you coming to my house to meet my parents?" Connie often asked.

"When we can do it the proper way," I replied.

Connie was still at school when I started dating her, and she usually spent the weekend at our house after leaving boarding school on a Friday afternoon. But one Saturday morning, her father, Gilbert Maloka, went to collect her from boarding school.

"I'm sorry, Mr Maloka, but Connie isn't here, she's gone to her auntie's house in Majaneng," he was told.

Like any concerned father, Mr Maloka set out to find his missing daughter.

Connie was in the kitchen making breakfast with my mother when she glanced out of the window and saw her father walking up the path that led to our house. She rushed to my mother.

"Please, Mma, don't tell my father I came here on Friday. He will be very, very angry with me!"

"I have been told that my daughter is staying at your house," Mr Maloka said, clearly restraining himself as he peered over my mother's shoulder.

"Yes, welcome to our house," my mother smiled as she opened the door. "Connie comes every Friday, she spends the weekend with us; she is a wonderful child – she is just like one of my own." My mother offered Mr Maloka some tea, and he rather stiffly sat down. I had also expected Connie's father to be angry, but soon he was caught up in conversation with my mother. He did not seem to notice our discomfort. In time, I was invited to Connie's home, and her family were warmly receptive towards me.

With mid-year exams looming, I put all my efforts into studying and spent every weekend on campus; I was determined to pass all my second-year subjects. One morning I was walking up to the canteen to get something to eat when I noticed a scuffle on a playing field. I barely gave it a glance, and the rest of that day I carried on with my daily routine. But the following morning, the campus was tense and a student stopped me on the walkway.

"There's a meeting at 7 o'clock tonight, make sure you're there," he said.

"What's it about?" I asked.

"It's about the student crisis," he said before hurrying off to pass on the news to a nearby group of students.

"Are you coming to the meeting?" Eddie Moloto asked when I passed him in the hallway.

"I can't, I've got a test tomorrow. What's it all about?" I asked.

He shrugged his shoulders, apparently uninterested. But I was curious, so I decided to attend the meeting after all.

Anyone who has ever attended a student gathering at Turfloop will understand what frustrating time-wasters those hastily organised meetings could be. There didn't seem to be any organised leadership as there was no longer an SRC, and students shuffled into the hall in dribs and drabs. There was certainly no fixed agenda. I made small talk with a couple of my friends, but I soon grew impatient, and I was about to leave when Oupa Mathlare called out to me.

"Hey, Herman, don't leave now, the meeting's going to start in a few minutes."

A group of students started singing liberation songs, swaying and chanting in the cold hall while we waited for the meeting to begin. I was anxious to return to my room and resume studying, and even though I wanted to see what the meeting was about, I could stand the delay no longer. So I took it upon myself to stop the singing and get things moving.

"Okay, guys, be quiet," I shouted to the crowd. I stood up and faced them as the chanting died down. "Who called this meeting, and why are we here?" These were questions that everyone wanted answers to, and to my surprise I ended up chairing the meeting.

To find out what was going on, I asked each student with a

grievance to present their version of events. It turned out that the scuffle I had noticed the day before was an altercation between members of the university's football team and disgruntled students who were opposed to its existence; members of the football team hit back at their detractors, and the meeting became quite heated and chaotic.

"Okay, let's be calm, people. We'll give both sides a chance to present their case," I said. But the atmosphere became volatile, and soon afterwards a comment from one of the footballers triggered a walk-out. Once outside, the disgruntled students vented their frustration by going on the rampage: buildings were torched, including the dormitories of some of the football team members.

Pandemonium reigned throughout the night, until the darkness was invaded by the white headlights of police vehicles that surrounded the campus. The atmosphere was tense. I was too afraid to return to my own dormitory, so I spent the night in a room where I hoped the university security officials would not find me. The decision to hide was instinctive; it turned out to be a wise one, as many arrests were carried out during the night.

With exams underway, most of the students were anxious to return to their studies and resume classes. But the following day another mass meeting was called, and this time the entire student body was in attendance.

"They can't just come here and detain all these students! It is unacceptable!" a voice cried out to cheers of support.

"Are we going to submit to this treatment, or are we going to stand against it?"

It was clear that we needed a body of representatives to negotiate with the authorities to release the detained students, and so we duly elected a steering committee.

I was elected as a member of the committee. I was the youngest and only a second-year student myself, so it was with some reluctance that I accepted the position. But I'd realised that someone had to take charge. It was, ironically, my calm demeanour that pushed me into the limelight – people generally shy away from loudmouths, maybe because they tend to be unpredictable and lacking in credibility.

The newly elected student committee drew up an agenda, and we approached the rector of the university with our grievances. We consulted with him, listened to the solutions that he and the university council put forward, as well as their complaints, and then we took these to the students. Over the next few days we went back and forth, back and forth, between the two parties. Gradually, though, we began to realise that the university council had no intention of resolving any of the students' grievances. The student committee made several presentations to the university council, but our requests fell on deaf ears. After a tense week, during which time classes were suspended and there were regular confrontations with the police, it became clear to us that the strategy behind the closure of the university was to break our morale and for the police to continue with their arrests without any student interference.

The campus conflict raged for a week, and then one blustery autumn morning I awoke at 6 o'clock.

"The campus has been surrounded by armed policemen in Casspirs; they're just waiting for us to incite a protest so that they can get us with their rubber bullets and teargas," Oupa said.

We managed to remain calm throughout this difficult time. The university authorities advised us that it would be safer for everyone if all students returned to their homes. They also said that we could expect correspondence notifying us about how we would move forward from this impasse.

I returned to my room and quickly packed my clothes and as many of my personal items that I could comfortably carry. I wanted to get off campus before dissatisfaction boiled over into anger and a demonstration. It was with immense frustration and disappointment that I had to leave the university, and I felt terribly uncertain, not knowing as I walked away whether or not I would ever return to the place from where I eventually hoped to qualify as a political scientist.

Back in Hammanskraal, I messed around for a couple of weeks, catching up with old friends and playing the odd card game. I also cooked meals for my aged maternal grandmother, who loved nothing more than having her family fussing around her. My cousin often joined me when I visited her, and together we would clean her house; it was a pleasure doing these chores as she smiled with gratitude and joy.

My grandmother was blind, and she lived in nearby Majaneng, a very under-developed rural area. She relied on her R7 quarterly pension – which barely covered daily living expenses. Her son, Uncle Boy, was a builder who lived in a tin shack on her property. He was a good builder, but he lacked discipline. Uncle Boy would secure a local building job and then, if a client was foolish enough to pay him before the job was complete, he would stop working on it and find another job somewhere else. My poor grandmother had to deal with disgruntled clients who came to find out why Boy hadn't completed their building projects, even though they had paid him. She also had to support Boy on her miserable pension during the periods when he wasn't earning. Because of all this, she was grateful to have our company and help, as Boy never made any attempt to help with the daily chores.

These visits to Majaneng helped pass the time during the excruciating wait for the university's letter to arrive. When the official envelope did eventually arrive, I tore it open, eager to read its contents.

"What does it say?" my sisters asked, crowding around me.

The letter was a serious blow to the future I had mapped out for myself. The university council warned that unless students adopted an attitude of commitment to their studies and undertook to adhere to the university's rules, we would not be welcome to return to campus. But I read between the lines; I knew what that letter really meant.

"It says that unless I am prepared to sacrifice my dignity, I can forget about continuing my studies," I said, unable to keep the bitterness from my voice.

As I folded the letter and put it back in its envelope, I knew that I would not be returning to the University of the North; I would never have to walk past that monstrous cement coat of arms at the main gate, with its motto, "Die mens se hand."

Although I no longer wanted to be a student at a university that ruled its students with an iron fist and treated them disrespectfully, my decision was not taken lightly. I still wanted to earn a degree, but apart from this I had a financial obligation not only to my sister and her husband, but also to the bank and St Peter's Seminary. That period of my life was difficult and confusing: I felt disappointed, demoralised, angry and depressed. For a brief period I feared that my usual optimism might degenerate into complete hopelessness. Maybe I had not realised the full truth of what my friends and Pobane had been saying all along – that life was extremely difficult for a black man.

If I gave up my studies, I knew that I would have to find a job that would enable me to pay back all the money I owed to those who had put their faith in me and supported me. I was divided between wanting to study, so that I didn't fall into the trap of the hand-to-mouth existence experienced by many of my friends and my brother, and paying off the student loan. But my greatest desire was to leave the country to join Umkhonto we Sizwe – the pressure was overwhelming, and the temptation to escape that oppressive environment was enormous. During those long, idle days I spoke to various groups of friends who were also considering going into exile.

"My uncle knows someone who can get us out; we can go and join the cadres in Tanzania," one acquaintance offered, while another said, "I'm going away so that I can fight the boere; you can come with me if you like."

I felt strongly committed to joining the struggle. At home, I paced the floor in frustration, hoping and waiting for an opportunity to leave. But I grew increasingly demoralised and impatient, and I finally realised that none of the promises I'd been made were going to materialise into actual arrangements to leave South Africa.

I decided that I would have to work. I would have to button my lip and do the unthinkable: take a job with the white man.

Chapter 9

The chilly days stretched into the bitter winter weeks of 1980. The sheer monotony and inactivity of the long days made each idle week indistinguishable from those before and those that followed. The unproductiveness of this period was soul destroying. The newspapers mirrored my feelings of depression as they reported on the country's continuing turmoil. There were demonstrations and boycotts across the country, and headlines screamed out: "School Demos Reach Crisis Levels." There were predictable reactions: "Enter the 'New Nazis'" as the Blanke Volkstaat Party was founded by right-winger Eugene Terre'Blanche; and "Sasol Blasted by Terrorists" reported on Umkhonto we Sizwe attacks on Sasol and the national refinery.

Throughout this bleak political period, the government continued its reign of terror, as police arrested people and held them for long periods without trial, as they had been doing since the 1960s. The only ray of light was Bishop Desmond Tutu – Secretary General of the South African Council of Churches – who joined the Anti-Apartheid Movement in its campaign to release ANC leader Nelson Mandela. The campaign was supported by many anti-apartheid groups, both locally and internationally.

Despondency greeted me when I awoke each morning, but I was reluctant to reveal my sense of depression to anyone. My family had always been so supportive of me, how could I betray them now, making them feel that their faith in me had been misplaced? I did not want to upset them. So, whenever anyone asked me, "How are things going?" I'd smile and say, "Fine, everything's fine. I'm working on getting a job; it won't be long now."

The harshness of that winter was relentless, but after I awoke every morning, washed and dressed, I put on the smile I needed to get me through the day, trying to convince myself that if I remained positive, an opportunity for employment would materialise. I was terrified that if I allowed the black cloud of depression to settle upon me, I would never be able to escape from underneath it; afraid that if I did not get properly dressed, I would not be presentable enough to pounce on whatever opportunity might present itself.

My family had always reached out to assist me, and during that gloomy period they continued to believe in me and offer support. My brother-in-law, Joe Moumakwe, who married my sister Florah in 1981, sent a message to inform me that there was a job going at a Spar distribution warehouse in Hercules, Pretoria. In spite of wanting to work, I experienced conflict. During this period, the South African Council of Churches was promoting study opportunities for black students to study abroad. I wasn't sure if I wanted to leave the country to pursue a military training programme, or to get a bursary from the SACC to study. And I still had serious reservations about working for whites. After careful consideration, I decided to apply for the job at Spar and tried to suppress my racial prejudices against whites.

I took great care to appear presentable, and I was waiting outside the Spar before the doors opened, sitting in the empty car park, watching as white employees arrived. The Spar warehouse was a busy distribution centre that supplied groceries to Spar supermarkets in Pretoria and the surrounding areas.

During my interview, the human resources manager rattled off a list of duties I was expected to perform: "Check invoices against outgoing deliveries; check the outgoing deliveries against the delivery notes," and so on.

I knew that I was more than capable of the menial duties that the manager would assign to me, but still, I tried not to show my relief and joy when he offered me the job as a despatch clerk. My salary was R180 per month.

I caught the daily train from Hammanskraal to Hercules, proud at last to be a contributing member of society and to be in a position to prove to my family that their faith in me was well placed. In reality, my duties consisted of shuffling papers; the work was uninspiring and unfulfilling, and I soon came face to face with the petty racism that I'd expected and dreaded having to deal with. The warehouse manager was an elderly man called Van Geffen who mistrusted anybody who was black; the black staff tolerated his insults by patronising him during their interactions with him, or belittling him behind his back. They realised that Van Geffen's fragile ego was easily stroked by addressing him as Baas Van Geffen, in this way avoiding his wrath. There was no doubt that Van Geffen's attitude was sanctioned by management, because whenever a report was made against him, it always resulted in the complainant getting a raw deal from Van Geffen at a later stage.

I continued to avoid conflict, though. When I was growing up I was seldom involved in arguments or fist fights; I avoided conflict at all costs, and Louis still jokes with me, "I've never seen you in an altercation of any sort; Herman, you are the master of conflict-avoidance." Whenever I observed my friends argue among themselves or with figures of authority, I realised that emotional or physical retaliation only exacerbated the situation, whereas withdrawal, or a well-timed joke or smile, defused the situation and saved everyone from a confrontation that would probably be forgotten in a few hours, anyway. I knew I had to adopt the same non-confrontational attitude while working at Spar if I was going to continue working there, and so when a spiteful person said or did something unkind, I either laughed it off or ignored it, reminding myself that I did not want to join the ranks of the unemployed again.

It did not take me long to realise that even if I worked overtime and did more than my share of work, Spar would employ me as their despatch clerk indefinitely – there was no opportunity for advancement for black employees. However, I did realise the value of being employed, and I continued to work with enthusiasm and diligence. Through it all, I kept up my usual interaction with people, confident that a better opportunity would come my way if I was patient and receptive. My attitude was rewarded seven months later when I managed to get a job as a clerk at Motani Industries.

Motani was a modest furniture manufacturing company in Koedoespoort, outside Pretoria. Owned by Omar and Satar Motani, the company manufactured fine furniture, and had just launched a lounge suite range in quality fabrics and leather when I started working there. I was employed in a similar dead-end job to the one I had at Spar, but the situation was more tolerable because I experienced none of the racist harassment that I had experienced at Spar.

During our tea and lunch breaks, away from the sawdust and incessant noise of the factory, I met and interacted with the rest of the staff. While we ate and drank, I listened to what other people were talking about, and I soon came to appreciate the value of listening; in this way, I picked up a lot of useful information.

While I was employed at Spar, I became fairly good friends with a colleague, Ismail Ibrahim, an amiable man who enjoyed banter about everything from PW Botha's inflexible approach to governance to the fighting style of Charlie Weir, the world boxing champion from Durban.

One day, Ismail and I were sharing our personal dreams and he said, "Herman, you've got too much potential to work here for the rest of your life, you should go into business for yourself." We discussed various ideas that we both had, and during one of our conversations he mentioned a cousin who seemed to have his finger in a lot of pies. "My cousin regularly rents community halls and holds concerts in them; he earns quite a lot of money from these promotions," Ismail said.

It was 1982 and I was already in my second job, with no real prospects of making a meaningful career for myself. I thought long and hard about my discussions with Ismail, mulling over the information I had picked up, and hoping that I would hit upon the right career or come up with an inspiring idea that would allow me to live an independent life.

"What's the matter?" Connie asked whenever she saw me get a faraway look in my eyes.

"I just feel like I'm on a treadmill, doing the same boring stuff over and over again, and that I'm never going to get off; if I don't find something that excites me soon, I think I'll go crazy," I said.

Connie faced me and folded her arms around my neck, her lovely eyes looking into mine.

"The right opportunity will present itself, my dear. But you must be patient. Just continue to be alert and positive, and something will turn up," she said.

I wasn't always reassured by Connie's words, but I was always soothed by her calmness and patience.

At least my work frustration was somewhat balanced by the lifestyle that Connie and I enjoyed. After completing high school, Connie had taken a job with Southern Sun as a bookkeeper, and we both looked forward to weekends when we socialised with our friends and family. It was infuriating that we had no access to whites-only cinemas; that we could only visit the Pretoria Zoo on appointed "black" days; an, that we had to confine our dancing and socialising to friends' houses or shebeens instead of the glamorous and hip whites-only clubs in town. Still, we managed to make the best of our leisure time – it was our pressure release from the stress of working in a white man's world. Weekends were, usually, forty-eight hours of hard partying.

During the weekdays, I worked hard, but at night I tossed and turned sleeplessly, frustrated that I did not have a big idea for a business that would enable me to realise my dream of being in charge of my own destiny. It angered me that there was no chance at Motani of earning more if I worked harder. But I couldn't dwell too much on the future because I had immediate responsibilities. I had almost finished paying back my student loan and I wanted to marry Connie, which meant that I would have to pay lobola for her.

I never rushed into things without careful planning, so, once I had paid off the student loan, I decided to ask Connie's parents if I could marry her. Representatives from my family met in the traditional way with representatives from Connie's family, and we completed the formalities involved in the payment of lobola: Connie's father agreed on an amount of R800 – which I paid in June, 1982. After this, Connie and I started planning our formal white wedding.

I had always dreamt of owning a car, and at last I decided to make the dream reality. White South African theatre audiences had been captivated by the 1974 musical *Ipi Ntombi*, which featured the velvet-voiced Margaret Singana. The show went on to become an international hit, and in 1980 it returned to South African stages after a sell-out season in New York. Although blacks were barred from attendance at theatres in white areas, some theatres had begun to relax their attendance criteria, and I so I was able to see the show at the Alhambra theatre in Johannesburg three times. I was captivated. "Ipi Ntombi" means "where is the girl" and the musical tells the story of a migrant worker living in the city and his girlfriend in a faraway village.

I phoned Louis and said, "Louis, you've got to come and watch *Ipi Ntombi*; I've got an idea."

My idea was to take the show to the townships, and I decided on Soshanguve as the place to start, to test the waters.

"Where the hell do you think you'll get enough money to put on a show like that?" Louis said, visibly appalled at what he saw as my recklessness.

"I'm going to make a plan; this is a big opportunity," I said.

I remembered Ismail's cousin who hired out halls for entertainment, and I decided take my own shot at the big time. I made an appointment to see the manager of the Alhambra Theatre, where *Ipi Ntombi* was playing, and tried not to show my surprise when he agreed to meet me.

Next day, when I walked into his office, my suit felt too tight and my mouth felt too dry to say the words that needed to be said. I swallowed, smiled, and stuck out my hand to shake his.

"I have watched *Ipi Ntombi*, and it's a story for the townships. It's been a huge success with white audiences, but it's time that black audiences got the chance to see something they can identify with," I said.

The bemused manager pointed at the chair opposite him, and motioned me to sit down.

"Look, Herman, I admire your initiative. But I need more motivation if I'm going to uproot the whole cast and pack up the set and send it all out into an untested market."

I leaned forward and looked hard at him. "Sir, where I live, people are starved for entertainment. And if there's one show they deserve to see, and that I know they'll love, it's *Ipi Ntombi*," I replied.

To my astonishment, the manager stood up and shook my hand. "Okay, we'll give the show a trial run of three nights at a hall in Soshanguve, and once we've gauged the response from the audience, we'll discuss further engagements."

We clinched the deal without any paperwork or contract of any kind. Just the promise of a R3 000 deposit, which was the sum total of my savings. I felt as if I was floating as I left the theatre; I was filled with confidence, amazed that I had simply asked, and my request had instantly been granted.

Ipi Ntombi would be performed over the Easter weekend. I employed Louis as the production manager, and the first night – Good Friday – opened to an appreciative, yet very modest, audience. But on the second night there were barely enough people to fill the front rows. The cast were furious, and we cancelled the rest of the performances. I realised that my enthusiasm for the project had got in the way of efficiency. I had not managed the project properly: instead of overseeing the project every step of the way, I had delegated duties and hoped for the best. I had paid people to put up posters to advertise the event, but I had done very little else in the way of marketing the event. I had nobody but myself to blame for the disastrous experience, and I lost the entire deposit. Worse than that, I felt humiliated. I decided that the next time I undertook a project, I would take full control of all the stages, without relying on others to ensure its success.

But there were other things that preoccupied me at the time – and foremost among them was Connie. The primary reason for wanting to marry Connie was simply because I loved her. But I also knew that my partying could not continue; by marrying Connie, I hoped that my life would calm down, and that I would no longer be caught up in such a fast, unstable lifestyle. Though Connie may have hoped for a husband who was content to live an average life – a husband who had a steady job, at a bank or somewhere similar, where there were prospects of gradual promotion – she soon realised that I would never embrace mediocrity. I wanted a big life, and I needed Connie to be the stabilising force of our marriage.

Although I was engaged, my friends still perceived me as an untiring party animal, and while Connie never objected to my socialising, I felt that I had outgrown that delinquent stage of my life. I was ready to embrace adulthood and its responsibilities. But my friends refused to let me off the hook so easily.

"Come on, Herman, what's the matter with you, aren't you allowed to go out and have fun with us any more?" they asked.

"Is Connie the one who is boss in your house?"

I was happy to agree that Connie ruled our relationship, because I had a plan. With Connie earning an income, the time seemed ripe for me to break away from the nine-to-five, mind-numbing work at Motani Industries. I hoped to find a job in sales, where my earnings would reflect the effort and number of hours I put in; the allure of big commissions was tempting. But to be a salesman, I knew that I needed transport. And almost nobody in our village owned a car.

I started saving again. I was well aware that my partying friends would commandeer any car I cared to buy, so having Connie at my side was the perfect excuse. Every man knew that once you were in a relationship, the woman called the shots; I would be expected to calm down and spend more time at home instead of partying.

Feeling confident of my plans, I shared my ideas with Connie. "I want to look for a job where I can earn commission." I took her hand in mine, and said, "I could earn high and I know that the work I put in will show when I get my cheque at the end of the month."

Connie looked at me a while before saying, "Ja. It sounds like a good plan. But what sector are you thinking of – cars, insurance, direct clothing?"

"I am not sure," I admitted, "but I know something will come my way."

Connie listened carefully as I outlined my dreams of being properly rewarded for hard work, and she eventually agreed that I should leave Motani. I was careful not to share everything with her, though. I feared that her common sense would prevail, and that she might try to delay my plans.

One Saturday morning, I woke her up early.

"Get yourself dressed, Connie, we're going shopping," I said as I leapt out of bed.

We enjoyed regular trips to Pretoria, where we usually

did some window-shopping before having lunch at Captain Doregos. However, when we arrived in Pretoria that morning, I steered Connie away from the city streets and shop windows, and led her towards the taxi rank. There, we caught a taxi to Laudium.

"Why are we going to Laudium?" Connie asked, a frown of disappointment on her face.

"We're going to look at some cars," I said.

"Isn't that premature? You can't even drive yet," she said, doubt narrowing her eyes.

I didn't allow Connie's practicality to dissuade me, though, and after some gentle cajoling I was able to persuade her to accompany me to Laudium.

A while before this, I had mentioned to Satar Motani that I wanted to buy a car. At the time, I relied on trains and buses to travel to and from work, and the fixed transport schedule made it impossible for me to work overtime.

"Herman, I can get you a special deal. When you're ready, let me know. I'll put you in touch with a friend of mine who owns a Toyota dealership," said Satar Motani.

"I'm ready right now," I said.

He wrote out his friend's dealership details: Kharbai Motors, Laudium.

"Okay, take this and go and look at the showroom. If you find a car you like, my friend will give you a good deal," he promised.

That Saturday, Connie and I stood in the forecourt of Kharbai Motors, where sunlight glinted off the windscreens of new cars. Holding hands, we walked up and down the rows of new cars, our eyes scanning the price tickets displayed on the windscreens. We couldn't resist running our hands along the striped or checked blue, grey or brown car upholstery, with its brand-new smell. Inside the showroom we stopped. In front of us stood a shiny blue Toyota Corolla – priced at a whopping R6 800.

The salesman was attentive, and when I told him I worked

at Motani he disappeared for a while before returning. Then he sat down at a desk and informed me that he had instructed the onsite finance company to work out a payment schedule based on my salary, which he had verified with Motani.

Connie looked agitated and pulled me aside. "Why did you let him do all that work, Herman? You should tell him we're only browsing," she said, clearly embarrassed that the salesman had put in so much effort when we weren't even there to buy a car.

"Look, we can afford it, and with a car there is no limit to what we can achieve," I said, determined to own that brand-new car. Not entirely persuaded, she walked back to the salesman.

In less time than it had taken to travel to the dealership, I had signed the purchase documents and the car licence application. The salesman handed me the car keys.

I had never driven a car in my life, although I had often watched taxi drivers changing gears, while thinking, "That looks easy, I can also do it."

Connie's eyes darted about with anxiety as she softly pleaded, "Herman, please, let's catch a taxi into Pretoria and pay a taxi driver to take the car back to Hammanskraal for us."

Ignoring her, I climbed into the driver's seat, inhaled the new smell of the car, and switched on the ignition. The car jerked forward, and it took a couple of minutes and a bit of manoeuvring before I managed to engage the clutch and put the car in first gear.

The salesman rushed across the floor and said, "Mr Mashaba, are you sure you can drive?"

"Yes, of course, I'll be fine," I smiled.

The Corolla hiccupped out of the dealership like an old drunk. My palms were sweating, my mouth was dry, and Connie yelled and wept alternately; the tension was terrible as I struggled to engage gear. Every time we approached a stop street or a robot, Connie stiffened as I tried desperately to hit first gear, so that we wouldn't have to judder across another intersection in fourth.

My shoulders ached with tension.

By the time we reached Hammanskraal we were able to converse without clenched jaws. I knew that Connie was proud of our new purchase when she suggested we visit my sister, Conny, who was a nurse at nearby Jubilee Hospital, to show off our new car. My sister was shocked and delighted. "A new car! Hey, Herman, how did you manage this?" She sat in the driver's seat, held the steering wheel, and adjusted the rear-view mirror – just as I had when I first got into the Corolla. When Conny's tea break was over, we said goodbye and prepared for our journey home.

I had never reversed a car. I stared at the gears, located the reverse position, and engaged the clutch. I was over-enthusiastic, though, and applied too much pressure to the accelerator. So we reversed – right into a tree. When we arrived at my mother's house, she was as pleased with the car as Conny was, though her delight was soon tempered when she saw the ugly dent in the shiny chrome rear bumper.

Once the afternoon's tensions had been smoothed over with a cup of tea, Connie turned to me and calmly said, "You need to take driving lessons, Herman – and the best place would be one of the driving schools in Pretoria."

"But why should I pay them all that money?" I said. "You know that my cousin is a bus-driver. He can teach me." And so my unfortunate cousin, who was also conveniently a neighbour, spent the rest of the weekend teaching me to drive.

When I thought about the traffic on the road to Koedoespoort, I did not feel confident enough to drive to work on the Monday. But by that Tuesday I felt I had practised enough to take the car to work. From then on, during the long daily trip to Motani, I spent my time thinking about my next step towards independence.

Two months after buying the Toyota, I passed my driver's licence and managed to get insurance, which was just as well, because I was involved in an accident in a few months later, in

November 1982. We had to spend Christmas without the Toyota, as the panel beaters were closed over December.

During this time, I reassessed my future. Soon afterwards, I made an appointment to meet Satar Motani.

"I wanted to hand in my notice personally. I am leaving Motani," I announced. "I want to thank you for giving me the opportunity to work here."

Satar Motani looked surprised. "Are you unhappy?" he asked.

"No, it's not that at all," I replied, not quite knowing how to explain.

"Has someone been unkind to you?" he persisted, puzzled that I was leaving if I wasn't unhappy.

"No, Mr Motani, I think I'm just too hungry to settle into the comfort of an ordinary job; I want to pursue my own business career." I said.

He nodded his head and said, "I wish you well, Herman. You deserve good luck."

It was extremely gratifying that Satar Motani and most of my colleagues wished me well. Leaving the company in such a dignified way allowed me to maintain an enduring relationship with the Motanis, one that remains strong to this day. Many such long-lasting business and personal relationships have stood me in good stead down the years.

During lunch breaks at Motani, I regularly scanned the newspapers and perused the adverts. I often wondered what the advertisers meant when they posed the question: "Do you want to be a millionaire?" Of course I wanted to be a millionaire – but I also wanted to know what I needed to do to earn that kind of money. The insurance industry was renowned for opportunities it offered to earn big bucks, and I decided that I wanted my share of it all. So, after twenty-three months' service at Motani Industries, I left and joined a well-known insurance company, hoping to increase my earnings significantly.

"Please remember that I only earn R400 a month. This only

just covers our basic expenses," Connie said. We weren't yet married, and I could understand her need to remind me of the reality of our situation. I could always rely on her to keep my head from floating too far above the clouds but, still, I refused to consider the option of a dead-end job for the rest of my life.

"Connie, I know you're anxious about our financial security, but a sales job is the only way I can set my own salary. I don't want anyone else deciding what we'll achieve for the rest of our lives," I insisted.

While Connie had grave doubts about my decision to resign from Motani, she nevertheless stood behind me. Her own dreams for our future were as big as my own, yet she seemed instinctively to know that there was room for only one maverick in our relationship; and that one of us had to feel the ground under their feet.

Chapter 10

A wedding is a joyous event, and Connie and I took great pride in planning our own. Connie spent weekends choosing her bridal gown, her bridesmaids' dresses, and deciding on the formalities of the day. A few days before the wedding, I decided that if I were to do one thing to look like a respectable groom, I should try to do something with my crazy wild hair, so I decided to have a perm. My hair had always been coarse and unmanageable, and I wanted to look my best for our special day.

I entered the hair salon with trepidation, but the place was alive with excited chatter among the hairstylists and the clients, and filled with the pleasant scent of lotions and shampoos and conditioners. When the stylist had completed the perm treatment, I was delighted with the silky texture of my hair; I never imagined that my unruly hair was capable of being tamed.

Our wedding was eventually held in February 1983 in Seabe, the village where Connie had grown up, and all our friends and family were at the celebration. Connie wore the white dress that all brides dream of; she glowed, and I felt privileged to be marrying my beautiful best friend.

It was our plan to pay a visit to my village to introduce Connie as my wife, but we were so heartily welcomed when we arrived in Majaneng that we changed our minds – also, this gave Connie a chance to wear her beautiful wedding dress for a few extra hours. We enjoyed an impromptu second party with my family and friends, who provided great music and platters of beef, chicken, salads and vegetables. Alcohol flowed as we all partied.

Little children ran up to Connie and touched her dress, her veil, her gloves; their dusty toes touched her white shoes, and as Connie indulged them, the children reminded me of the time I was a member of the marching band that played at weddings, a time when we were in awe of any bridal couple and their retinue.

Once the wedding was over, we turned to planning our life together. Home ownership was almost impossible for black people at the time, however. The government was not building new houses in townships, and even if a piece of land was for sale, we had to pay cash as financial institutions had redlined black residential areas.

Before Connie and I got together, I used to sleep in the dining room in my mother's house. There were only two bedrooms in the house, one of which was my mother's. Nancy and Florah slept in the other one. I realised that I could not take my bride to a bed in the dining room, so Connie and I purchased a small ZoZo hut that we erected at the back of my mother's house. It was only about four square metres in size, but that little wood-and-iron hut was our own private place – an adequate arrangement for a newlywed couple who were content simply to be alone together.

We had planned to go to Durban for our honeymoon, and one day Connie came home from work glowing with excitement. "Guess what? I've managed to book a room for us at the Maharani Hotel in Durban at a reduced staff rate!"

As soon as we had saved enough money, we drove down to Durban in our blue Corolla, and spent a week there. This was not the kind of thing village people did back then, and my family just shook their heads. "First a car, and now a honeymoon in Durban! What's next, Herman?"

Leisure travel was unheard of in those days – few black people owned cars, and even fewer went honeymooning on the Durban beachfront. Mostly, people only travelled long distances to attend to family matters – lobola negotiations, weddings and funerals; they certainly weren't in the habit of heading for whites-only beaches.

The Maharani was one of only a few hotels that admitted black guests at that time. The pristine Durban beaches were officially off-limits to blacks, except on Boxing Day, but there were no racial restrictions on the beach directly opposite the Maharani. Hand in hand, Connie and I crossed the road and strode onto the beach. We stared out across the rolling waves of the Indian Ocean, feeling the warm water pulling at our ankles. We had only ever seen photographs of the ocean, and we revelled in the feeling of the sand between our toes, the loud rushing of the waves and the foam that spread across the beach. Connie blocked her ears. "It's so loud!" she shouted.

Although it was rare at the time for restaurants to serve black patrons, a nearby restaurant did allow black diners, and we were on our way there one evening when an elderly white woman stepped in front of us and said, "Why don't you people stay with your own kind?" Connie and I sidestepped her without replying; we refused to allow the racial prejudice of strangers to ruin our honeymoon.

We took advantage of all the Durban sights and experiences that we could afford, including, of course, the few activities open to blacks. We stood at Durban harbour amidst the squawking gulls and drank in the salty smell tinged with fish and diesel from tugs chugging around larger boats. We stood in the queue next to the Dick King statue on the Gardiner Street Jetty at South Beach and bought our tickets for the boat trip on the *Sarie Marais*, thrilled to be enjoying the experience in each other's company. Our honeymoon trip may have been instrumental in our becoming ardent travellers; that visit to Durban opened our eyes to the extent of our country, and we realised that perhaps, after all, GaRamotse was not big enough to warrant a dot on a map.

I soon landed back in reality, and realised that I had made an error of judgement in taking the insurance job. I did not receive adequate training from the company but, still, I followed up on every lead that I was given. One day I arrived at a woman's house in Mamelodi township, Pretoria.

"Welcome, Mr Mashaba," she said. While she made some tea, I looked around her modest dwelling – the basic furniture, her brood of children – and as I sat there trying to convince her why she should part with a large percentage of her limited earnings, I had a revelation. I did not believe that the insurance policy was what she needed at that moment in her life, and I felt as though I was taking food out of the mouths of that woman's children. The woman reminded me of my own mother, and when she sat at her tiny table, listing all her expenses, I knew that every cent she earned was badly needed by her family. In good conscience, I could no longer sell insurance, I did not feel connected to the product and I did not have the passion to be enthusiastic about it. And without the passion, I instinctively knew that my chances of being a successful insurance agent were slim. It was an enormous setback because I had bought into the hype that surrounds the insurance sales industry without fully considering the product.

Once again, I turned to the newspapers. I went through each advertisement, circling sales positions, and phoning to enquire about the products or services offered by the companies. After talking to one of the telephonists, I learnt that a company in Pretoria North called Lessan was looking for a crockery salesman.

A state of emergency existed in almost every big township in South Africa at the time, and PW Botha was the dictatorial State President. Black men were routinely stopped by police.

"Where are you going?" they would demand. "What are you doing here? Are you here to cause trouble? Where did you get that car?"

The harassment was intimidating – I knew it was inevitable

that at some time I would be stopped and interrogated. Freedom of movement was severely restricted, but I minimised the risk of arrest by dressing well and knowing which big corporate companies had offices in the areas where I worked. Whenever I was stopped by the police I was pleasant and always called them "baas"; this generally placated them and, if it didn't, I told them that I was employed at Barclays Bank or the biggest company in the area. When they glared at me in disbelief and disdain, or sniggered, I offered to take them to the company, where they could verify my employment. Of course, this intimidated them and, like typical bullies, they usually backed off with a weak warning.

Despite the emergency conditions, the crockery and cutlery sales went well. But, still, I felt that I was capable of more.

"I've had enough of this crockery and cutlery. I'm going to look for other products too," I said to Connie.

"Why not try selling linen?" she suggested, giving me a smile. "I've seen for a while now that you need a new challenge."

I took her advice and signed up with a linen manufacturer. Soon I was selling a bedding bale as well as a full set of crockery and cutlery to my clients, and my earnings were climbing steadily. But once I had sold a linen set or a set of pots to a person, that was it, they were not repeat customers: I was not offering a product that people needed to replace every few weeks or months. This meant that I had to constantly travel to new areas, find new customers and generate new business. Because of the pass laws, my movements were restricted, and I could only operate in areas where there was a familiar police presence.

In addition to selling crockery and cutlery, I branched out even further and started selling fire-detection systems for a Swedish couple, Steve and Heather Gustafson. It was while working for them that I learned the art of salesmanship – techniques that ensured I got the sale. During the day I had to be disciplined and make appointments, because the more appointments

I made, the better my chances of success were. I travelled the townships during the mornings and afternoons, stopping off at houses and making appointments to return in the evening to do a presentation. It was pointless making a presentation without the whole family present, because it was necessary to sell the benefits of the fire-detection system to the whole family. The crucial thing was the fears of the family – if parents thought their children might be in danger of dying in a fire, they wanted the system installed. Even if homes did have electricity, many people relied on cheaper products such as paraffin for cooking and coal for heating, so the risks of a fire were very real in many homes. Connie often accompanied me on those appointments in the evenings; we worked well as a team.

I targeted primarily the more affluent township dwellers, and I was cold-canvassing in Mamelodi one morning when I arrived at a four-roomed house where a pregnant woman was scrubbing the floor.

"Good morning, I'm selling fire-detection systems," I said, closing the gate behind me.

The woman stood up and dried her hands. "Good morning, I'm Mary Itsweng. My husband is at work; it's no use showing me," she said.

"Maybe I can make an appointment to come back when he's home," I said, refusing to be put off. Mary seemed reluctant, but I persisted until she agreed to an appointment on the Friday evening.

Soon afterwards, Connie and I went along and we made the presentation; we did not sell the Itswengs the fire-detection system, but we did have dinner with them, and we subsequently became good friends. During that time, I made friends with a lot of people I met, and many of these friendships developed, and have endured. The crockery and linen sales were our bread-and-butter money, but the very successful fire-detection sales provided us with the jam.

Steve Gustafson was a generous man who became more than just an employer. To be able to work in other areas, I needed my work permit signed. Steve did so without hesitation or fuss, giving me peace of mind and allowing me greater mobility. I continued in this way, representing three or four companies at any given time; but my big break came one morning after I had dropped Connie off at work in Sandton City in Johannesburg.

I was poring over the real estate section of the newspaper, looking for a house to buy in Soshanguve, near Pretoria. My eyes were blurring from the same boring two-bedroom-one-living-room ads. I turned to the Employment Offered column and noticed the advertisement for a sales representative for SuperKurl, a company that manufactured black haircare products.

I remembered how pampered I'd felt when I had my hair permed for my wedding and I knew that black hair products were products that I could sell. I hurried to a local café, where I changed a banknote for some small change; then I dialled the number in the cramped public phone booth.

The company owner's wife introduced herself as Mrs Thompson, and said to me, "Mr Mashaba, we were actually advertising for a white salesman." I felt disappointed, but thanked her anyway. Then, after a pause, she continued, "But come and visit our factory anyway, and my husband can interview you."

On the drive through to Malvern, Johannesburg, I passed through the busy centre of Johannesburg where taxis hooted and dodged their way in and out of traffic. This was unfamiliar territory, and I felt apprehensive about working for a company south of Johannesburg while I was living in Pretoria. There was not a morning I left home that I did not carry the risk of being arrested for a pass offence; it was exhausting, as the risk was so great. The last thing I wanted was to land up in jail! I had never been locked up, and the horrors that my friends had told me about were too nightmarish to contemplate – the brutality of apartheid jails, where blacks had no rights.

Once I arrived at the factory, though, my misgivings were forgotten. The place was a hive of industry, with machines spitting out lotions and potions, threaders sealing bottles, and conveyor belts delivering different-coloured bottles to packaging stations. Colleen Thompson introduced me to her husband, Leon, the owner of the company. He took me on a tour of the factory and then invited me into his office for refreshments. Over a cup of tea, he explained SuperKurl's areas of operation and I realised that I had at last found products that offered sustainable sales. But, most importantly for me, SuperKurl was a brand I believed in at a time when salons were mushrooming all over – in villages, townships and cities.

No further mention was made of the fact that SuperKurl were looking for a white salesman. Colleen said they wanted a representative to operate in Tembisa on the East Rand, and Leon invited me to join the company on a commission-only basis. My commission represented only 30% of the wholesale price, but I accepted his offer because I felt comfortable with the arrangement and knew that to a certain degree I was in charge of my own destiny – whatever effort I put into selling the product would be rewarded.

The following day, I accompanied one of SuperKurl's reps to Germiston and Katlehong to learn more about the haircare industry. The experience was overwhelming. Both black and white entrepreneurs were part of the new and exciting industry. Every salon we visited was packed with customers waiting to have their hair permed or relaxed. Later that afternoon, we returned to the factory and Colleen gave me product information and tips; she also handed me some order books so that I could hit the road on my own.

I was soon so involved in SuperKurl that I did not have time to juggle all the other products I was selling, so I decided to focus fully on my new job. In less than a year, I was SuperKurl's top salesman. If the white staff had any reservations about the new black salesman, they kept their feelings to themselves. I was punctual for sales meetings and presented my daily orders timeously. I was committed to the job, and I formed strong relationships with my customers. I was also assigned a full-time professional hairdresser – Sheila Setshedi, from Tembisa – who worked with me.

With my Corolla loaded up with samples, I visited salons in the area and found that I was quite comfortable in the world of black beauty. The rate of repeat business astounded me; I had no sooner delivered a product than I would receive a call to deliver another order. I'd got into the industry at the right time: black haircare was burgeoning, and informal salons were springing up on every street corner. Hairdressers are gregarious by nature, and I was always welcomed into the ammonia-scented salons with a smile and a cup of tea or coffee.

"Herman, what have you got for us today? Come and sit down, let me give your hair a treatment." This really was a very pleasant environment to work in.

There was more than enough business to go around, so I recruited an old workmate, Joseph Molwantwa, to join me at SuperKurl. I'd met Joseph at a time when we were both trading from the boots of our cars, I selling linen and crockery and Joseph selling clothing. Joseph and I became friends, and I regularly encountered him on trips into town as we sold to the same customers. He was also an impeccable dresser, and we had the same work ethic. But our sales approaches differed: where I turned on the charm, Joseph turned on the pressure – and it worked for him.

SuperKurl had many white sales reps, but the white market was small in comparison to the black market. Things went really well for Joseph and me, and eventually I became the top sales guy in the company, with Joseph a close second.

The sales environment suited me very well, and I was returning home each month with an ever-increasing pay cheque. Leon Thompson seemed to be impressed with my diligence, though he was possibly even more impressed with the fistfuls of money he was earning. As a result, he and I embarked upon a road trip to neighbouring African countries to introduce SuperKurl. On the long stretches of road we discussed business matters, and Leon mentioned that he was concerned that his chemist, Johan Kriel, might be planning to go into business on his own.

Johan Kriel was a respected chemist in the beauty field, having developed beauty products for Reeva Forman and Avroy Shlain, two large direct-marketing beauty companies in South Africa. He had also worked for Revlon South Africa for many years. Not only was he a highly competent chemist, Johan Kriel was also a gentleman who engaged with all the staff at SuperKurl.

It had become clear to me during my working experience that some white employers didn't have any allegiance towards their black staff, and had no compunction in firing them. And although I was successful at SuperKurl, it bothered me that Leon had invited his brother-in-law to join him in establishing a new brand called Magic Curl. I realised now that I'd have to carefully consider my future at SuperKurl.

Connie and I were living very comfortably, and she must have breathed a sigh of relief that I had at last found my niche. But although I was content with my life, I knew that there was something more for me. I didn't just want the gold watch when I retired from SuperKurl in twenty-five years' time; I wanted to own the gold mine.

Chapter 11

Christmas 1984 was approaching. December is the month when South African businesses traditionally close down for their annual break, and many white employees escape to coastal towns where sea breezes revive their spirits – Durban, Port Elizabeth, Plettenberg Bay and Cape Town. It is also a lucrative time of year for retail business and, like many employees, I looked forward to receiving an annual bonus so that I could pamper my family during the Christmas festivities. As usual, Leon Thompson and his family went on their annual vacation, and he left his brother-in-law to take care of the business.

During this busy period, the SuperKurl range of products seemed to walk straight off the assembly line onto the salon shelves; production could barely keep pace with the demand from consumers. I spent those long summer days in my un-airconditioned Corolla visiting township salons, taking orders or delivering them. Then, squinting against the sunset, I returned to the company with fistfuls of cash, handing it over to the admin personnel, who in turn handed the money over to Leon's brother-in-law. SuperKurl was making between R100 000 and R200 000 a day in cash sales.

Like me, most of the SuperKurl employees had to forgo a vacation. We had to work to ensure that we could fulfil the Christmas orders. In appreciation of our loyal service, Leon arranged a braai in his absence – a party to thank his employees and to ensure that we felt some measure of festive spirit.

I had slotted into the black haircare industry with ease, and

I felt confident that I now had a good understanding of the industry. I had already mentioned to Joseph that I felt we could create our own black haircare company, but he was financially comfortable and had doubts as to who we might employ to create our product range. Connie and I were enjoying a lot of socialising and travelling, and so money was not the sole motivator for me. I wanted to own my own company – and in the back of my mind, Leon's misgivings about SuperKurl's pharmacist, Johan Kriel, lingered.

Unlike Joseph, I was not content with just being comfortable, so I pulled Joseph aside one day and said, "Leon suspects that Johan Kriel may be leaving SuperKurl to develop his own business interests."

"So? How will that affect us?" Joseph asked.

"Well, if we can persuade him to join us rather than going on his own, we'll solve our problem of finding someone to formulate products for our own range," I replied.

In 1984, blacks and whites very rarely had any kind of social interaction, and it was certainly unheard of for a black man to approach a white man to join him in a business. But I knew that if Joseph and I had any hope of succeeding, we needed Johan. Joseph and I had many discussions on the matter, and Joseph was generally rather sceptical.

"Instead of Johan joining us, I think we should approach the black production manager," Joseph said. "He works with the product – he must know how to produce it," Joseph said. He was afraid that if we poached Johan, it would cause problems between Leon and us. I agreed, and we had several meetings with the production manager. Very soon, though, we realised that he was merely a mixer and had no technical expertise or knowledge about what chemicals were used in the formulas. So we had to exclude him from our plans as he could add no value to our new enterprise. By this time, we knew that the only person who could help us was Johan Kriel, and the end-of-year

SuperKurl braai would be the perfect opportunity to approach him.

The appetising aroma of meat sizzling on the braai and the sound of beer bottles clinking added a sense of camaraderie to the festivities, and I approached Johan. He was an amenable man and engaged readily in conversation.

After some pleasantries, I said to Johan, "Joseph and I have got a plan. We're thinking of leaving SuperKurl and going on our own."

Johan listened without saying anything, and yet I recognised a fellow entrepreneur and I could see that his mind was racing ahead with the possibilities that my vision presented. Eager to capitalise on his interest, I said, "All of us – Joseph, you and I – would be equal partners with equal shareholding in the company."

At that stage, I had absolutely no idea about how much funding we would require for the new company, or even where we would get funding from, but I knew that the essential ingredient was getting Johan on board: we needed someone who had the chemical expertise to develop a product range.

Johan fetched another drink from the bar and called me aside.

"Herman, I'm flattered by your offer and I would like to join you," he said. "But I am in a difficult position – my family is related to Leon and I have to be cautious. I don't want to be seen to be betraying family. I hope you understand,"

I understood his dilemma, and Joseph and I left the Christmas party somewhat deflated.

However, Johan's sense of allegiance soon dissolved when Leon returned from holiday. He thanked Johan for his commitment to the company during the holiday period, and then handed him a rather meagre annual bonus. This inevitably worked in our favour, as Johan was insulted that his loyalty to SuperKurl was rewarded in such an offhand manner. But it was not only the insignificant bonus that upset Johan; it was also Leon's failure to deliver on his word to make him a partner in the business.

Feeling doubly insulted, Johan phoned me and said, "Do you still want to start that company?"

I could barely conceal the elation I felt. He went on to tell me that he would join us in forming a new company – but he had one condition. "Herman, I must tell Leon that I have been offered a partnership; I don't want him hearing it from anyone else."

This put Joseph and me in a predicament, but Johan promised not to disclose who he was going into partnership with. He duly informed Leon of his dissatisfaction with his employment conditions at SuperKurl, handed in his resignation, and asked Leon if he expected him to work out his notice or to leave the company immediately. Leon was upset by these developments, and immediately set about trying to dissuade Johan. He also tried to find out who Johan was going into business with.

At the time, Johan and his wife were living at his mother's home in Boksburg. There was a rather odd incident one morning when Johan was leaving for work. He noticed a car speeding up the road towards him, and as it came to a brief stop, the occupant stuck his head out of the window and stared at the house. Johan thought the man was lost, perhaps trying to locate an address in the area, but before he could approach the stranger to offer assistance, the man sped off. Johan didn't think anything more of it, and drove off to work.

The SuperKurl factory was a busy enterprise, and it was customary for employees to step out for a short break during the day to break the monotony of the noise and the bustle. It was part of Johan's routine to take a mid-morning break and walk down to the café, where he would buy a pack of cigarettes. As he stepped out onto the sidewalk outside the SuperKurl factory, he noticed that the same car that had stopped outside his mother's house that morning was parked across the road; the driver was skulking behind a newspaper, apparently trying to conceal his presence. Johan realised that he was being followed.

He was furious, and suspected that Leon might be behind this invasion of his privacy, but he was too angry to confront Leon. So he stormed back to the factory, fetched his car keys, and left SuperKurl. Johan was outraged that he had openly informed Leon of his intention to leave SuperKurl and yet Leon was having him followed. He drove home, fuming at the realisation that he could no longer trust Leon.

When Johan had started working for SuperKurl, Leon had promised to make him a partner and to include him in other business enterprises that he was involved in. But now it was clear to Johan that every time he had asked Leon to formalise their partnership or to give him the promised shares in the company, Leon had provided him with a weak, evasive excuse. By employing a private investigator to follow Johan, Leon had ruined the relationship. And so Johan phoned me and said he'd be willing to join Joseph and me in our new business venture. But nothing was signed and sealed yet.

Johan's wife, Christine, was to play a major role in persuading him to join us. For despite what had happened between him and Leon, Johan still felt torn between family loyalties and the chance of owning his own company; during the moments when he vacillated, Joseph and I felt quite desperate. We knew that he was key to the potential success of our new venture, and the idea of his remaining with Leon was too much of a risk. So we took the decision to visit Johan's home in his absence.

Christine Kriel welcomed us and listened to our persuasive pleas, and she proved to be instrumental in encouraging Johan to be firm with Leon and to join Joseph and me. It would be a lie to say that either Johan, Joseph or I left SuperKurl with the blessings of the company. Indeed, Leon was outraged at our departure.

When Leon initially heard of our plan, he called me to his office for a frank discussion about his suspicions concerning Johan.

"I know you're going into partnership with Kriel, but I think you should rethink your alliance – how can you trust him? If he's so willing to leave the employ of his family, how loyal do you think he will be to you and Joseph?" Leon said. "Johan will go where he gets the best offer. You will always have to look over your shoulder – if he is offered a better deal, he'll leave you and Joseph on your own. And the two of you will never manage without him."

There was an uncomfortable silence as I weighed up what he said. I could offer no response.

"I can tell you now that you and Joseph will never make it on your own," Leon went on. "You boys are dreaming; you know nothing about business."

Leon's strategy was to discourage me from associating with Johan. He insinuated that Johan was unreliable, untrustworthy and lazy. But I recognised Leon's badmouthing for what it was – a desperate attempt to keep us all under his control. When Leon realised that his strategy wasn't working, he turned on Joseph and me. After a brutal discussion, Leon knew that I would not be deterred from my path, and that I was prepared to accept the consequences of my decisions. As far as I was concerned, I had nothing to lose by pursuing this venture, and I was more determined than ever not to reverse my decision to make a go of things on my own.

I had the key people necessary to start the business, but the spark I needed was funding. I immediately thought of Joseph's friend, Walter Dube; he owned a distribution company called African Agencies, which imported black haircare products from Atlanta in the USA. But a local competitor, a financially strong white-owned company, had approached Walter's American principals in the mid-1980s with a view to being the local distributor of their products, and Walter lost his licence to import the products. As a result, there was a big gap in the industry just waiting to be filled.

Being privy to this information was useful, and I felt that Walter's predicament might propel him into considering funding our new business. In addition to Walter's financial capability, I also knew that he had insight into and expert knowledge of the industry.

Walter Dube is an entrepreneur. As a young man he had trained as a car mechanic, and the first R6 he earned by fixing someone's car he immediately used to kick-start his entrepreneurial career. By the time I met him, he already owned a petrol garage and a shopping centre in Mabopane. Joseph and I had the first of many meetings with him in his small office at the petrol garage. The garage serviced the taxis in the area, and the forecourt was spattered with diesel and oil, which had bonded with the sand that blew off the untarred roads in the area.

Walter was a gracious host and listened as Joseph and I described the business we had in mind. Because of his experience in the black haircare industry, Walter listened attentively to our ideas. But he soon got down to the nitty-gritty. "Where's your business plan?" he asked. Joseph and I looked at each other rather sheepishly.

We returned a day or two later with a business plan, supported by a comprehensive record of sales at SuperKurl. Every time we visited Walter, he would ask us business-related questions that helped to tweak our business plan until he was finally satisfied with our feasibility studies.

"How much will you need to get the business up and running?" he eventually asked.

Johan had worked out exactly the amount we needed for the start-up.

"Thirty thousand," I said.

"I'll lend you the money on the following conditions. I must be a 25% shareholder in the company; you must pay interest at prime plus 10% on the loan; and all three of you must also each provide R3 000 cash as security." Walter looked hard at us as he said this, but he also had the hint of a smile.

The loan conditions were generous, and I could barely contain my excitement. But there was a problem: although Joseph and I had the cash, Johan didn't have any savings at all. Even so, Walter accepted the R6 000 and granted the loan. The relief I felt at securing that start-up loan was immense; step by step, I was creating the reality that I had envisaged for myself. That small boy in Hammanskraal with holes in his shoes would finally get to stand on his own two feet and walk the path he had always dreamed of walking.

With the funding in place, I knew that we could start the business. But we still had to have many meetings with Walter – we had to introduce Johan to Walter, to work out where we would operate from, and what we would call this new company. During one such meeting, we decided to meet the following day to discuss possible names for the company. We duly arrived the next day with a couple of names written down. Walter is a well-travelled man and an avid reader, and he recalled having read the book *Black Like Me* by John Howard Griffin. The book tells the story of a young white American man in the Deep South in the 1950s; he was acutely aware of racial tension at the time, and wondered what it would be like if he were black. Griffin bought skin-blackening chemicals from a pharmacy, and when his skin darkened he embarked upon a trip around the southern states of America as a black man, experiencing the oppression and racism he had seen black people endure.

"I think 'Black Like Me' would be a great name for our business," Walter said, and we were unanimous in our decision to adopt the name.

What appealed most to me about the name was that it suggested black pride, a consciousness of what our new company aimed to promote, and what it would offer to consumers. Johan initially felt that Black Like Me was a rather in-your-face name for a black company operating in a white-dominated society, but he eventually supported it when we convinced him that we were appealing exclusively to the black market. With consensus about the name reached, Johan set about looking for premises for the business.

I was tasked with developing an image for our new company. TCB Academy in Johannesburg was the top hairdressing training academy at the time. I had become friends with two of their employees, Lilly Plaatjies and Ella Matlejwane. These women used their knowledge of American marketing concepts and strategies to help me conceptualise and develop a brand identity for Black Like Me.

At the time, it was still illegal for blacks to own or operate businesses in white areas, so Johan was tasked with securing premises for us in Ga-Rankuwa – the area where my paternal grandfather had once worked as a security "boy". The advantage of having Johan as our business partner was enormous – he could go places where no black man could; he was the white face that our company needed in order to be established.

While Joseph and I visited salons, spreading the word about our new product range, Johan, with assistance from Walter, secured a 200 m² factory in Ga-Rankuwa, a low-roofed space in the Small Business Development Corporation (SBDC) business park. When I visited that mini-factory for the first time, my mind exploded with the vision of a busy company pumping out products for Joseph and me to sell. It was immensely rewarding to know that after all the years when I had been forced to hustle to get by, I would finally be the co-owner of a legitimate business that would allow me to provide for my family as a responsible citizen. Black Like Me was officially born on Valentine's Day, 1985.

Apartheid sought to separate races, and in doing so it entrenched suspicion between them. Trust between black and white was not a natural state, and although each of the partners had doubts about the other's loyalty, we just had to forge ahead, put our trust in each other and hope for the best. Johan was the only white partner, and he was understandably somewhat insecure about his position in the company. So, before formally agreeing to join us, he requested a partners' meeting.

"Chaps, I'll formulate the best possible products for Black Like Me; but I am adamant that these formulas should not be 'stolen' from SuperKurl. If you expect me to walk into Black Like Me with the recipes from SuperKurl, then I'm not your man. But if you want an equal, or even a better, product, then I'm the right person. I just want you to realise that I won't compromise my integrity," he said.

On our side, Joseph and I were a little sceptical about Johan's ability to create a product equal in quality to those manufactured by SuperKurl, but he nevertheless assured us that he could develop quality products from scratch. We spent many meetings discussing which products would be best to launch our range, and where we could maximise profit.

We eventually decided that it was necessary to produce a complete product range if we wanted to make a real impact in the market. At the time, the perm system was the most popular product among consumers. It consisted of a pre-softening gel (Step 1), a perm lotion (Step 2) and a neutraliser (Step 3). To complement it, we required a normal shampoo, a hair conditioner, a spray, and a curl activator: these would be our main launch products. We decided to produce the product range in different sizes. Johan devoted all his energy and time to mixing and testing until he was satisfied that he had superior products that we could confidently promote to the salons.

The perm lotion used by SuperKurl contained monoethanol-amine, a chemical compound that reacted with thioglycolic acid to form a relatively weak perm lotion with a pH of about 8.5; it was a product that hairdressers generally favoured. But monoethanolamine is a very expensive ingredient. Johan's experience in the beauty and haircare industry was extensive, and he had discovered that monoethanolamine could be substituted with ammonia; it was about one-tenth of the price of monoethanolamine, and equally effective.

Joseph and I had reservations about Johan's plan to substitute monoethanolamine with ammonia, but he assured us that the product would work. To prove his point, he mixed 5-litre containers of Step 1, Step 2 and Step 3, and suggested that we decant the samples and take them to the stylists.

"I'm going home now," he said. "If you and the salons are happy with the products, call me – otherwise, don't." Then he packed up and went fishing with his father.

I was nervous – what if the product was not on par with those of our competitors? But my fears proved to be entirely unfounded: the response from the salons was so enthusiastic and positive that my reservations dissolved and I phoned Johan, barely able to contain my excitement.

"We've got a winner!" I said.

We felt affirmed and emboldened, and so we pushed on. SuperKurl had a near-monopoly on the black haircare industry at the time. Revlon was also active, but their expensive products were tailored to serve the top end of the market. Our new product was so well received by salon owners and hairdressers that we felt reassured that Black Like Me would succeed in the highly competitive haircare market.

The product range that we manufactured was restricted by the affordability of the equipment we needed to buy. But Johan was as creative in his use of the equipment as he was with the formulas he devised for the products. With the R30 000 capital at our disposal, we bought chemicals and bottles and the most rudimentary equipment – a small platform scale, a single bottle filler, a 200-litre drum. In those early days we did not even have deionised water, so we improvised and used tap water. We manufactured the products in the 200-litre drum, which gave us enough to fill 800 bottles.

The tight control of our budget meant that we could not afford to hire extra staff, but we did employ one young handyman, Joseph Mogole; he was physically very strong, which made him suitable for the job of mixing the product. He also helped with bottle-filling. Joseph, Johan and I applied ourselves with energy and enthusiasm in the manufacturing process so that we could get the products out on time. Connie also helped wherever she was needed – though we had appointed her full-time to take charge of office administration.

On the day we took delivery of our first consignment of bottles, we made a batch of shampoo and decanted it. By 10 o'clock that morning, Joseph and I had loaded our cars with the product and Johan waved us off.

"If Joseph and Herman come back before the end of the day, we'll be okay. And if they don't, we know we still have a lot work to do," he said to Connie.

Joseph headed off to his usual area while I drove to my salons. At about 3 o'clock that afternoon, we returned to the factory; we had both sold our entire consignment – for cash. We were so motivated that we loaded up our cars again; what a rewarding moment that was!

Every transaction that took place was meticulously written up by Connie. We were all rather fearful of Connie – she was disciplined and efficient, and her wrath was something to avoid. From the outset, Connie had been supportive, but her commitment to the company was personal: she knew that anything that went wrong would have an impact on my dream – our dream.

Within seven months, Black Like Me had repaid its debt to Walter Dube, All the partners were earning well. Of course, we bought ourselves the luxuries we felt we deserved – fine clothes, new homes and fancy cars; but if we thought we could spend with abandon, Connie quickly brought us back to reality. Joseph, Johan and I were out on the road for most of the day, and it was inevitable that we sometimes slipped into a daydream and exceeded the speed limit. But Joseph was the worst – he was notorious for getting speeding fines. He felt it was acceptable to expect the company to pay his fines since he usually got them while out on the road on business. Connie, however, was having none of it; she decided that Black Like Me was not responsible for the partners' misdemeanours. When Joseph tossed outstanding fines onto her desk, she ignored them and refused to pay them.

It wasn't too long before a warrant of arrest was issued to Joseph for outstanding fines, and when he returned to the office after appearing in traffic court he was furious. "I put my fines on your desk; you should have paid them!" he said to Connie.

"I'm sorry, but Black Like Me won't pay for personal speeding fines; the company isn't going to absorb costs arising from bad driving," she replied in her placid manner. No amount of gentle persuasion would get her to budge from her non-payment policy on traffic fines. It was this kind of resolve and commitment to running the company professionally that made us all realise that Connie always had the interests of the company at heart.

Inevitable obstacles and challenges cemented the foundations of the partnership in the new business; during these difficulties, we all came to realise that we were doing our best for the company and that we could trust each other.

Our first major order outside the Gauteng area came from East London: a R25 000 order from Andile Jamela, our agent in Mdantsane in East London. It was a massive order, and the customer wanted it filled almost immediately. We were a new company, and understandably the customer was rather circumspect about our promise to deliver. But on our side we were concerned that we would send the product and not get paid for it. The order was one we could not afford to pass up, and I thought of a way to break the impasse.

"We three will deliver the products personally, in our bakkies," I said to my partners. Forging a relationship with the customer would ensure future orders that we wanted and needed. So we arranged to meet the customer in King William's Town, and from there on the transaction went smoothly. Joseph and I had arranged to spend a week with Andile in East London to help promote the products, and Johan drove back to Pretoria after delivering the order. After just a few days in the area, visiting salons and demonstrating the product, we managed to sell most of Andile's stock. It was a win-win situation for both parties, and we looked forward to returning to the Black Like Me factory to prepare an even bigger order to ship to him.

At the time, Connie was overwhelmed by the huge local demand for stock. She urged Joseph and me to get back as soon as possible, so we drove back from East London and sent our delivery vehicles back to Pretoria by rail.

Our intention had been to focus on one geographical area at a time, to saturate it with our products and build it up before moving on to the next area. But fortune smiled on us, and the products had grown wings that we'd have been foolish to clip.

Johan admits that in the first year of business he was reluctant to write down the Black Like Me formulas. He felt that at any time we could turn around and say we no longer needed him, so he hung on to the secret formulas until he realised that his doubts were groundless and that we weren't going to dishonour our agreement with him. It was just as well we reached this level of complete trust, a trust that has endured and grown into a deep friendship, because when Black Like Me started gaining on SuperKurl, we had to deal with Leon Thompson. He had set out on a campaign to discredit us.

When we started our company, SuperKurl's perm lotion was selling for R83, and we budgeted that we could sell the same-sized perm lotion for R78. Thompson competed with us by sending his reps to the salons to promote a "buy one, get one free" offer. So, during a staff meeting about this I said, "Okay, let's go head-to-head and offer the same deal." But Black Like Me was hampered because of our limited equipment; SuperKurl had the advantage over us of having the equipment and the staff to churn out massive quantities of the product. However, Thompson made a bad mistake in miscalculating our commitment to our company.

Perm lotions are usually thickened with cellulose, so the way we made the lotion was to boil water in the 200-litre tank and then sieve in 5 kilograms of cellulose; the mixture had to be cooked until it thickened, and then allowed to cool. This slow method of production was a great disadvantage in our attempt to equal SuperKurl's offer, but we refused to be beaten. Johan and Joseph brainstormed how to get around this, so that we wouldn't be knocked back by SuperKurl.

"Maybe the solution lies in our turnaround time," Johan suggested, and proposed conducting an experiment.

"Let's try putting cold water directly into the drum and then adding the cellulose. Then we allow it to swirl, and then add a couple of grams of ammonia, and then we put all the other chemicals in," he suggested.

We had nothing to lose, so we tried this immediately. Thankfully, Johan's innovative plan worked, cutting down the production time and allowing us to compete against SuperKurl – proving that we could produce our quality products in a factory twenty times smaller than theirs.

As is the case with every new business, it's impossible to factor in all the contingencies and setbacks in a business plan, because many of these difficulties arise only once you get started. But having Johan's expertise and resourcefulness was a major boost in keeping staff spirit buoyant – and, indeed, in keeping the business afloat – when many may have given up. Those early days proved that we were all fighters, and we faced the challenges that arose with calm optimism and a dedication to building Black Like Me into a major contender in the black haircare product market.

Thanks to apartheid policies, our factory in Ga-Rankuwe was off the beaten track, as I've mentioned, and its remoteness made access to many clients difficult; this was compounded by the fact that there were no telephone lines in the area. Being unable to communicate with our clients was stressful and frustrating, and as a result Joseph and I made sure that we were in daily physical contact with our clients. The upside of all this was the face-to-face contact that is essential to the maintenance of client relationships.

Black Like Me was making money like a Monopoly game, and Johan was our "Get Out of Jail" card. The Ga-Rankuwa industrial area had been established about ten years before, and the Bophuthatswana National Development Corporation had their offices opposite our factory. Johan took on the task of getting telephone lines installed. He went to see officials, wrote letters to the phone company and completed the necessary forms, and within six months our business telephone was installed. It was a step up the ladder of professionalism for the company, and clients could now phone in their orders to Connie. This freed up Joseph and me, and we focused on expanding our client base.

A state of emergency had been declared in parts of South Africa in 1985, and it was extended throughout the 1980s; these were dangerous and depressing times to be working in the townships. Police and soldiers were seconded to the country's major townships, where they patrolled the streets; they were a threatening menace in a hostile environment. Funeral vigils were held for people who died during the violence, and the presence of the army and the police force created tensions that time and again flared into yet more violent outbreaks. The killing was a vicious cycle.

It was in this hostile environment that Joseph and I tried to sell the Black Like Me products. Home became my sanctuary, the place where I could escape the acrid black smoke of burning tyres, barricades and hostility – experiences that I encountered almost daily.

Joseph and I continued on our daily rounds in that turbulent environment, visiting salons to deliver and take orders. At the same time, Johan visited suppliers. His method erred on the side of caution as he didn't want any of the suppliers to get an idea of what our product formulas were, so he purchased each of the materials from different suppliers, which presented a logistical challenge. We were run off our feet, but youth has energy on its side and we coped with the stress of the new business.

Once I started to enjoy the benefits of the financial success of the company, I wanted to keep up the momentum. I struck out to improve the marketing, hoping to make Black Like Me a market leader. There were times when my partners shook their heads at some of my unconventional ideas, but I persisted nonetheless, and the company's visibility grew.

Black Like Me was in the beauty business, and in 1985 we decided that we wanted our marketing to reflect this. "We need to get Black Like Me on television," I said to my partners, and we set about making this happen. In 1986 I started negotiating with the SABC about establishing a product that would be mutually beneficial, and that same year Black Like Me made a large investment in its first major TV campaign. We sponsored a 13-part hair and beauty grooming series that educated viewers on all aspects of personal grooming.

The response from the industry and the public was overwhelming, and the programme was such a success that before the first series had finished airing, the producer called me and said, "Mr Mashaba, the SABC has commissioned an additional 26-part follow-up series."

This programme was the foundation of a long and rewarding relationship with the SABC. Ironically, this success came during the time when the national broadcaster was controlled by the old regime. But despite this, the top management of the SABC gave the company an important break, and we developed a working relationship. We were all businessmen, despite the fact of our being cast as black businessmen and white businessmen.

Bessie Louw, who was the manager of all the SABC TV stations, was an outstanding executive who supported initiatives with business. She made it clear that the collaboration between the SABC and Black Like Me represented a new vision for South Africa. "Black Like Me represents how the future South Africa ought to be," she said at one of our meetings. I doubt that anyone at that meeting had any idea how happy I was to hear this, because I have always striven for non-racialism.

The support and understanding we received from the SABC had the effect of opening my eyes to my prejudices. My unyielding opinion that all whites were racists who didn't consider the welfare of blacks had been challenged by Bessie's attitude, and I had to acknowledge that maybe it was time for me to get rid of my preconceived ideas.

When I was still working at SuperKurl, I used to call on the top hair salon in the Carlton Centre, and there I met Anver Saferdien. He was one of the most popular hairstylists in Johannesburg at the time. His passion for his profession and his flamboyant personality endeared him to his clients and associates. I knew that Anver could teach me a lot about the industry, so I made an effort to get to know him. We spent many good times over drinks, chatting and trading stories.

After a while, I decided to approach Anver about taking up a consultancy position with Black Like Me – I knew he'd add pizzazz to the company's marketing department. Anver accepted the offer, and the first thing he did was insist on a company launch at a well-known club in Johannesburg. He then went about inviting the glitterati to the event. What a spectacular hair show it turned out to be! Anver's innovative ideas prompted me to offer him a permanent position with the company, and a year later he joined the marketing division. He promoted our product range to hairdressers and did an outstanding job of writing articles that kept Black Like Me in the media spotlight. He marketed our relatively small company in such a way that we came across as being far bigger than we in fact were. But there was a flip side to Anver's charm – his fiery temperament, which made him one of the more colourful figures in the company. One thing I admired about his personality was the fact that if we disagreed, he didn't just roll over to make me happy – he always got me to consider an alternative point of view. Anver was a principled man who stood firm. I was prepared to overlook his – and anyone else's shortcomings – as long as I knew they had the best interests of the business at heart.

By the early 1990s, Black Like Me had developed an excellent relationship with the SABC – it was so good, in fact, that we were called upon to sponsor many different programmes and events. One of these concerned super middleweight boxer Dingaan Thobela ("The Rose of Soweto"), whose next fight was to be in the US. The SABC had won the coverage rights, and they approached Black Like Me to sponsor the fight – an amount involving R500 000. This was a lot of money, but in return I negotiated R1 million worth of airtime, which they agreed to. Our association with the SABC was cemented after this, and Black Like Me sponsored several other fights, including British heavyweight contender Chris Eubank's title fight in South Africa. I attended the fights with colleagues and friends, but my only involvement with the sport was as a sponsor and a spectator.

National television coverage was a huge boost for the company. But we also realised that being visible at a grassroots level was just as important, so we sought out marketing opportunities that would ensure a business profile.

The Zion Christian Church enjoys massive support among blacks in South Africa, and at Easter time hundreds of thousands of followers make a weekend pilgrimage to Moria, near Polokwane. When the SABC approached us to partner them in providing road safety measures over the weekend, it was obvious that this was an ideal opportunity for Black Like Me. So we hired a helicopter and also sponsored ground support crews. Branded in our black-and-white company logo, both the helicopter and ground support ensured that road safety was at the forefront of motorists' minds along the route. The Black Like Me brand was spectacularly visible in a very worthwhile cause – but it had also blazed an advertising trail for black-owned companies in South Africa.

Chapter 12

Good business practice ensured that Black Like Me prospered, and in 1986 Connie and I were in a position to buy our first home. When we'd first moved to Ga-Rankuwa in January 1985, we rented a neat three-bedroomed house in Zone 1, but a few months later a new housing development in Unit 8 was initiated, so we took the decision to buy our first house. The house cost R30 000, which was expensive at the time; it was in an upmarket part of the township that was close to our factory. It was the usual three-bedroomed starter home with a kitchen, lounge and bathroom. I added a garage, walled the property, and paved the outdoor areas. We lived there until 1988, when I sold it to a neighbour for R82 000 in the booming township housing market.

Not everyone was as fortunate as Connie and I were, though. My mother was still living in the rented house in Temba; she had never owned a home in her life. This bothered me, and I said to Connie, "I'd like to buy my mother a house. It know it would mean a lot to her."

A year after we'd bought our own home, Connie and I were able to buy my mother a house. It was a meaningful gift to my mother – being a homeowner was something that she could never have aspired to on her tiny wage. I had begun to realise that having money is like travelling – you cannot enjoy it on your own. I wanted to share my good fortune; it is in the shared experience that things become special.

Black Like Me was growing at a rate that not even I, in my wildest fantasies, could have envisaged. After just a year in business, production was so high that we had to consider moving out of the five mini-units we occupied in the Small Business Development Corporation business park. Johan had come to me and said, "Herman, we've got a problem. We're feeling the pinch in these tight premises, and we need to find something bigger."

"Can't we just rent the additional space in one of the neighbouring units?" I asked.

Johan shook his head. "I've tried. We've occupied every extra bit of space as it's become available, but there's nothing left," he said.

I was aware that staff were getting on each other's nerves in the cramped space, and fortunately the problem was solved when Johan found a 1 500 m² factory nearby. The move to bigger premises meant that we could purchase the new equipment we needed; we'd also be able to employ the extra workers we required to increase our output and meet the growing demand.

At about this time, Connie approached the directors about her workload. She had, up to then, taken the full burden of the financial and administrative duties on her shoulders, and she was feeling overwhelmed.

"We need to beef up our financial control, and I need more administrative support," she said. We took a decision to recruit an auditor, and soon afterwards we appointed Nisar Dawood. He closed down his auditing company and joined our executive management team as financial director.

The haircare industry was growing phenomenally in the townships, and no matter how many products we produced, there was always a demand. Once again, production outgrew our factory premises, and we were faced with finding an even larger factory. There was a high rate of unemployment as well as a skills shortage, and school leavers had very limited job opportunities. In this environment, hairdressing was an attractive and easy industry to enter, so hair salons were springing up everywhere.

After much consideration, I decided that we could not keep moving premises; the logistics were too demanding and it was not a sustainable path. I had a new idea, and after discussing this with the other directors, we decided that we needed to build a factory to our own specifications – one that was large enough to accommodate future growth.

Black Like Me was phenomenally successful, but still we could not find a bank to finance the building of the factory. Because of the situation, we began negotiating with the Bophuthatswana National Development Corporation (BNDC) for funding to buy the land we needed to build the factory. At the time, the Ga-Rankuwa industrial area was jointly controlled by the Bophuthatswana government and the BNDC.

One hot afternoon, Johan slapped a letter from the BNDC on my desk.

"Take a look at this. The only way we can get funding from the BNDC is if we buy the property through them, and they then manage our building project," he said.

None of the Black Like Me partners was comfortable with this manipulative method of doing business, so we decided not to pursue this funding route. A couple of months later, Walter Dube advised us to buy a property in a small industrial area in the middle of Mabopane, a mere 10 kilometres away from our Ga-Rankuwa factory.

The place was not without its problems, though, and Walter warned us, "There is no infrastructure, the roads are not tarred, and the lights often go out – even in a light rain shower."

We were torn between the need for expansion and staying where we were. But the latter would result in stagnation, so we took the decision to build a new facility in Mabopane.

The property acquisition took almost a year to finalise, but we were still faced with the problem of funding. Yet we couldn't just sit back and wring our hands, so we employed an architect Walter recommended, who went ahead and drew up plans. And instead of waiting for a loan to be granted, the company used partners' money to fund the building project. We moved into the new factory in 1989, and had already been occupying it for two months when we received a surprise but redundant notification: funding approval from the BNDC.

The company's move to an appropriately sized facility, and the excellent income the company was generating, inspired Connie and me to start looking for a house in a suburb that offered good infrastructure and which was situated away from the township disturbances I had to face daily during working hours. Influx control laws had been done away with in 1986, and petty apartheid was crumbling, despite, or because of, the ongoing political violence. In these difficult and unpredictable times, I wanted my home to be a safe retreat. So in 1987 we started looking around, and we were drawn to Waterkloof in Pretoria. The suburb was populated by embassies and diplomatic houses, which meant that it was a high-security area. I consulted my lawyers, who agreed to be the nominee as the Group Areas Act was still in force and I could not legally buy a property in a white area. The only way a black buyer could own a house was through a white nominee – a loophole that many wealthy blacks took advantage of at the time.

Connie and I settled for a lovely house that was one of the most expensive homes in the area. But before I could sign the papers, the government closed the nominee loophole which had previously "allowed" black ownership of property in white areas. We could have gone ahead with the purchase, but the threat of forfeiting the house if the purchase were discovered by the authorities deterred us. So we decided that, just as we had built our factory in Mabopane, we would build our dream home in Soshanguve.

We went all out, feeling that we deserved the rewards of our hard work. Connie and I had taken up tennis and we enjoyed playing with friends and family, so we built a tennis court. We also built a swimming pool, and we enjoyed many parties with our friends in our Soshanguve home. We lived the African dream in that house. Sure, we had issues with the bad roads that turned to sludge during the rainy season, and there was no telephone system. But it was a grand place to live in, with lovely homes and friendly, hard-working people.

It was during this time in Soshanguve that I visited Ahmed Kathrada, a few days after his release from prison; I went with my friend Goolam, who was related to the Kathrada family. A few months later, on 11 February 1990, Nelson Mandela was released from prison. I was at home with my family on that great day, together with visiting business associates from Chicago – we were negotiating to establish Debbie Howard's cosmetic brand in South Africa. We all watched Mandela's release on television, a moment I had never imagined I would experience.

We lived in Soshanguve until the early 1990s. A year after the release of Nelson Mandela and the unbanning of political organisations in 1990, the government scrapped the Group Areas Act. We were free at last to live where we wished, and because we had enjoyed living in a house of our own design, we decided to do so again. It was with much excitement that Connie and I hit the showhouse trail one Sunday, and started looking for land in Pretoria North, where smallholdings could be bought. We explained to the estate agent that we wanted to build our own house, but, sharp agent that he was, he mentioned a house in the area that was on the market, suggesting that we have a look at it.

We drove along the quiet acacia-lined avenues of Heatherdale, listening to the Piet-my-vrous calling to one another. As soon as the electric gate swung open and we saw the driveway winding up to the house, Connie squeezed my hand; we smiled at each other, signalling that we had found our dream home. The house was set on a 2-hectare stand, and it lived up to its driveway promise. At the price, the property seemed to be a bargain, so we made an offer that the owner accepted later the same day. We could not have been happier when the property was eventually registered in our name, and while we waited to move in, we spent many happy evenings planning the furnishings and dreaming of get-togethers with family and friends. But, yet again, our excitement was short-lived. One Sunday morning, our good friend Bra B – Kholekile Biyana – arrived at our home in Soshanguve with the Sunday papers under his arm.

"You just can't resist being on the front page, eh, Herman," he said.

"What do you mean?" Connie retorted, and opened *Beeld*. She spread the paper on the dining room table and we read about the furore brewing around our home purchase.

The government's racist laws had been scrapped, but people's racist attitudes persisted. It turned out that Mr Bentley, the previous owner of the house we'd purchased, had come to an agreement – prior to the sale – with other right-wingers in Heatherdale. They had agreed that none of them would sell their homes to a black buyer. However, the property market was not exactly booming when I made an offer on the said Mr Bentley's house, and since money usually has no colour if the price is right, the principled Bentley had apparently said to hell with the agreement he had with the other residents, and accepted my offer. Mr Bentley happened to own a small hotel opposite the property we had bought, and the zealous right-wingers marched to the hotel to protest against the sale of his house to a black family.

Koos van der Merwe, who is currently a member of the Inkatha Freedom Party, was one of those right-wing demonstrators, and in the same *Beeld* article he vowed that no black family would stay in Heatherdale for long, as he would make their lives miserable. In the same article, I learnt that the Minister of Foreign Affairs, Pik Botha, was to be my new neighbour – he lived in the house behind mine.

Connie was extremely concerned about all this. She pointed to the article and said, "Herman, we can't move to Heatherdale." With urgency in her voice, she reminded me, "Look how the police treated us in Hammanskraal. What will happen if these people threaten us when we move in? How can we rely on the police to protect us here; they don't want us here either."

I understood her fears and tried to placate her. "Connie, we have taken transfer of the property and we have to move in."

She started having nightmares about the right-wingers breaking into the house and killing us, and so I contacted a company to build a high security fence around the entire property. But I knew that this was not enough to protect us. There were other problems too – among them the planned upgrade on Connie's BMW.

I held out the BMW brochure she'd been looking at. "Connie, there's no way you can get a new BMW now; if you pull into the Heatherdale house in a shiny new luxury car, it will draw attention to us."

Connie was furious. She had worked hard and deserved to reward herself in any way she saw fit, but I wanted to minimise the impact of our moving into the neighbourhood. So we compromised by agreeing to purchase a black Jetta. Unfortunately, none of the dealerships I approached could source a black one, so I bought Connie a green Jetta instead. When the car arrived, she stood in the parking lot and stared at it, and I could tell from the thrust of her hip and the jut of her jaw that she wasn't happy. She fumed quietly for a few minutes, then she looked at me and said, "Okay, it is a new car. And many people don't have cars. It's fine."

I was relieved, but I was also grateful – as I had been countless times before – for Connie's positive attitude.

Life has a way of challenging our perceptions. Though we expected the worst from the militantly vocal right-wingers in Heatherdale, on the day we moved in things turned out rather differently. A prominent local Afrikaans businessman, his wife, and some of the other neighbours arrived to welcome us. And a few days later, while I was working in my office in Mabopane, my secretary buzzed me with the news, "Mr Mashaba, you have a phone call from Minister Pik Botha's office."

The phone call was an invitation to attend a "Welcome to the Neighbourhood" cocktail party. Of course we accepted the invitation, and local residents and the media were in attendance; both national and international newspapers covered the event, and the following day one headline read "Pik Welcomes Black Neighbours". Connie and I realised that the rest of the community had protected us from the minority group of right-wingers among them, and we were never bothered by anyone – right-wing or otherwise – in our comfortable new house.

Most of our neighbours were wonderful people; friendships we made in Heatherdale, for example with the Hough family, endure until today. And it was while living in Heatherdale that I voted in an election for the first time.

Although Black Like Me was a rising star in the late 1980s and early 1990s, and the partners were all making money, some of them wanted to branch out into other areas. In 1989, Joseph decided to sell his share in the business. When we'd started the company, we were totally inexperienced in business hierarchies, and as a result we didn't appoint a CEO – Johan attended to production, and Joseph and I managed the sales and marketing as equal partners. When we'd appointed Nisar Dawood as financial director, Joseph wasn't pleased. But Johan and I had managed to convince him that Connie needed the assistance of a financial expert if the company was to manage its money efficiently. Joseph had eventually agreed, but in the meantime he looked for other business interests. These business pursuits weren't of any real interest to me, but what did concern me were the weaknesses in our sales management. Because Joseph and I were equal dealmakers and rule-setters, a few wily customers took advantage of the situation. For example, I would get a phone call from a customer along the lines of, "Hi, Herman, can you let us have the hair relaxer at the same price we paid on the last order?" I would then call up their last order, and when I noticed that it was at the previous year's price, I would turn down the request. Unperturbed, the customer would simply phone Joseph and make the same request. Invariably, Joseph would approve the purchase, unaware that I had already turned them down. This kind of thing was losing us money, and I decided to call a special board meeting to discuss this weakness in our structure.

"Guys, I suggest that we split the sales and marketing responsibilities, so that we don't have two rule-makers," I said.

Joseph wasn't at all satisfied with the suggestion. "I don't see any reason to change our current system," he said.

It occurred to me that I had over-estimated Joseph's capacity to take on responsibility, and in my eagerness to foist a division on him, I had not properly evaluated his capabilities.

Instead of even giving my suggestion a chance, Joseph broke the news that he would be leaving the company. He'd given Black Like Me five years of good service, and it was a blow to me to hear him say this. I'd been with him from day one, and had always admired his drive. Eventually, we were forced to buy him out, and it was difficult to negotiate with a bitter person who took the position that we had pushed him out.

"Joseph, don't sell out," we urged.

"Leave your shareholding and enjoy the dividends," we said to him.

But he wouldn't be swayed.

"No, I want the cash," he said.

We had his shareholding evaluated, and I made him an offer I considered to be generous and fair. But he shook his head and replied, "No, that's not going to work for me."

He appointed lawyers to deal with his payout, and the deal the lawyers eventually agreed upon was substantially less than my original offer. I bought Joseph's shares and in time, as other partners also left, I bought their shares too.

Three years later, in 1992, Johan Kriel was the second partner to leave. He was an entrepreneur and a deeply committed family man. Black Like Me had given him the means to pursue other interests, and he had decided to sell his shares in the company.

"I'm going farming," he explained when he told me he wanted to sell his shares. Not long afterwards, he bought a beautiful farm near Emalahleni in Mpumalanga. Often, he'd phone me and say, "Herman, why don't you and Connie come out here and spend the weekend on the farm with us?"

Connie and I loved those farm weekends with Johan and Christine and their family. "It's such a relief to get out of the city," Connie would say, reclining in the passenger seat as we drove away from the week's stresses.

My parents, Matinte and Mapula Mashaba, on their wedding day in 1946.

A family celebration, mid-1960s; me (3rd from the right bottom row), my sister, Conny (2nd from left) and Esther in the background (right) in a jaunty beret.

My paternal grandfather Koos Mashaba, who named me Highman, with Aunt Elsie and her two daughters, Nurse and Nonnie.

My paternal grandmother Letta Mashaba (right) with her daughter Elsie and grandchildren Koos and Nurse.

A young Connie, years before we met.

It was 1979, I was in my first year at university, posing against a BMW which I one day aspired to drive.

The first time I saw Connie was at the 1978 Miss
Hans Kekana beauty pageant. I thought she was lovely,
and was proven right when she went on to win the
competition.

One of the weekends that Connie visited me at Turfloop in 1979.

1982. On the day I paid lobola to Connie's parents
we had our engagement party at their house in
Seabe. That's Esther celebrating in the background.

1982. The Bad Boys on the night of our engagement.

March 1983. Our official white wedding in Seabe.
Posing with my new wife.

Posing with my best man Louis at the wedding.

March 1983 in Esther's kitchen, having a post-wedding celebration. Top left to right – Kate, my sister Conny, Louis, my sister Flora, my brother Pobane and my sister Esther. Seated: Left to right – my cousin Shirley and my sister-in-law Salome.

One of the rare pictures of my brother, Pobane, which fills me with regret whenever I see it.

1983. Me in my first car, a blue Toyota Corolla, the foundation of my business career.

1983. Connie posing near my Corolla outside our first home in Temba.

1995. The two big influences in my life: Mr Gilbert Maloka, Connie's dad, and my mum, Mapula Mashaba, posing outside the house I bought for her.

1995. My mum holding my daughter Khensani, and my nephew Koketso.

1997. Connie with Khensani (3) and Rhulani (9 months) at our home in Heatherdale, Pretoria North.

Early 2000s. Gilbert and Enid Maloka, Connie's parents, with Rhulani, Khensani and my nephew.

The deposit slip of Walter Dube's loan to Black Like Me. It remains framed on my office wall to remind me of the start of my business journey.

The early days. Joseph, Johan Kriel and me outside the Black Like Me factory in Mabopane.

Connie and me at work. We eventually managed to install a phone line which revolutionised sales for Black Like Me.

Tony Lopez (centre), three times world boxing champion, with Walter Dube and me at the Sun City Superbowl in 1993.

Mid-1990s. Felicia Mabuza-Suttle on one of the occasions when she visited our offices after becoming a Black Like Me brand ambassador.

One of the major Black Like Me sponsorships was the SABC Road Safety Campaign helicopter in the late 1980s. I would often go up in the helicopter.

This picture of me and Bertie Lubner was taken on the day I joined the Field Band Foundation.

Prior to its public opening, we were among the honoured guests invited to a special event at Robben Island: Bill Cosby, Connie, Nelson Mandela and me in Mandela's cell.

Sharing a table with Hilary Clinton at the dinner on Robben Island.

2009. Shane and Celia Ferguson at my 50th birthday.
Shane has been my corporate adviser for many years.

Celebrating my 50th birthday at a Motown themed evening with
Connie on my arm.

Chapter 13

By 1993, Black Like Me was one of the leading black haircare brands in South Africa, drawing a lot of attention as the maverick company that had thumbed its nose at apartheid regulations. It came as no real surprise, then, when the company was offered R65 million by a multinational competitor.

"That sounds like an offer we can't refuse, Herman. You really should give it serious consideration," was Connie's response. We mulled it over, looking at the offer from all angles, but I eventually decided to turn it down.

"No, I don't want to sell," I finally told Connie – and the potential buyer too.

Instead of selling Black Like Me, I entered into a marketing deal with African Bank to train hairdressers, salon owners and distributors on the business aspects of the haircare industry. In addition, we ran a R500 000 competition for hairdressers every eighteen months, which focused on professional development within the industry. By this time, I had established Black Like Me regional offices in Cape Town, Durban, Johannesburg and Port Elizabeth, and I'd employed Lucas Sebobe as the head of sales.

The only thing still lacking in our lives was children. This was not for lack of trying – indeed, soon after we'd got married, friends and family had already begun to ask the inevitable question: "When are you going to have children?" Though both our lives were busy and interesting while I was still a rep for SuperKurl, Connie looked at me one day with a serious expression in her eyes. She said to me, "Herman, I want us to start a family."

Connie and I had travelled a long and difficult road together in our quest to become parents. During her first pregnancy Connie doubled over in pain and was rushed to hospital. She had an ectopic pregnancy and had to undergo surgery. It took her a couple of months to recover from the loss of our unborn baby, and although we didn't manage to conceive over the next three years, she was still positive that we would have children of our own. In 1984, a year after our wedding, we had felt blessed when Connie fell pregnant. Everyone had congratulated us, but our optimism was guarded because of our experience with the ectopic pregnancy.

"Don't be so anxious," the doctor reassured us. "Your worries are to be expected, but Connie's a healthy woman who takes excellent care of herself, and there's no reason not to expect a healthy pregnancy and a beautiful baby at the end of it." With the doctor's reassurance, we again began to look forward to the day that we would be parents.

But our expectations were crushed when Connie went into labour at six months.

"Herman, don't let anything bad happen to this baby; I couldn't go through another loss," Connie cried.

The doctor called me aside and told me, "Mr Mashaba, there's little hope of survival at this stage in the baby's development. You see, the lungs haven't developed sufficiently. And even though there's a very small chance that she'll make it, she may have many health problems." This was devastating news. The doctor proved to be right; our little girl didn't make it. After only sixteen hours of fighting, she gave up the struggle. Connie was heartbroken. I cannot even articulate how Connie's pain affected me; I have loved her since the day I first saw her, and seeing her suffer is one of the most shattering experiences for me.

Connie struggled to conceive again, and one day her mother said to her in desperation, "My child, what can you do to have a healthy pregnancy?" My mother, who was present at the time, tried to reduce the pressure on Connie by saying, "Herman didn't marry Connie for kids, he married her because they love each other."

Those words meant a lot to us – to me, because they showed that my mother knew how much I loved Connie, and to Connie, because she needed to believe that a child wasn't the cement in our marriage: what held us together was the love we had for each other.

After the loss of our daughter, Connie was referred to a doctor in Kempton Park and soon afterwards she underwent in vitro fertilisation (IVF). Unfortunately, it didn't work.

"I'm not giving up so easily, Herman; I am going to be a mother," Connie said, gritting her teeth and resolving to do whatever it took to hold our child in her arms. We were then referred to Dr Rodriguez at the Sandton Clinic, where Connie had fourteen more IVFs – but, again, none of them was successful. Our friends and family were very supportive throughout, and one day Louis Mkhetoni's wife, Sally, made an offer of real friendship.

"Connie and Herman, you are our greatest friends. We love you both dearly and we cannot bear to see the heartbreak of childlessness. I want to offer to be a surrogate mother for you," she said. Connie cried, and I could barely answer I was so overwhelmed.

Dr Rodriguez was positive about our chances of surrogacy succeeding. "I'll refer you to a counsellor who will speak to all the parties concerned. This is to ascertain candidacy for the procedure and the experience. Put simply, this means that if the counsellor approves you as good candidates, then I will refer you to a lawyer to draw up the legal contracts."

Sally conceived within two weeks, but in the third week of the pregnancy Dr Rodriguez confirmed that she had an ectopic pregnancy. This was a very hard moment for us all, especially Connie, who really took the failed pregnancy very badly. Soon afterwards I said to Sally, "You know I am very grateful for the generous gift that you have tried to give us. But, unfortunately, it is time to say 'enough'. Connie and I will just have to accept that we aren't meant to be parents. We have wonderful nieces and nephews and godchildren and friends' children – they are precious and we are blessed to have them in our lives. They will have to be our children, too."

Connie, who was exhausted and sad, did not disagree.

The years passed, and all our energy went into Black Like Me, whose extraordinary success exceeded our wildest dreams. Then, in 1993, Connie felt her biological clock ticking again, and she became broody. I have never resorted to traditional African doctors for any muti or advice, and I was quite taken aback when my mother suggested that Connie consult a traditional doctor she'd heard positive reports about.

"You can go if you like," I said to Connie, "but I'm not going with you."

Connie didn't have faith in traditional medicine either, so she was also sceptical. But she'd reached the stage where she felt she had nothing to lose and a baby to gain, so she agreed to go along with my mother.

Before she left, I said, "Sweetheart, here's the money for the doctor; but I don't want you to be disappointed. This problem isn't something that money can fix – if it was, you know I'd have given every single cent I own to give you a child. This is beyond our control, but I hope it works out for you."

Of course, the muti had no effect. Unfortunately, not everyone was as supportive as our family and friends, and one day Connie received a malicious phone call.

"Is this Connie Mashaba?" a voice asked.

"Yes," Connie replied.

"I wonder how you feel about your husband going to all these beauty contests?" the stranger said, unaware that Connie has never given in to the green monster of jealousy.

Connie coolly replied, "I don't know what you're getting at. It's part of his work. He's there in a professional capacity."

"I was just wondering how you feel about his being surrounded by beautiful, fertile young women. Especially since you haven't been able to give him a child," the stranger said.

Connie put down the phone and let out a sigh. When she told me about the phone call, I took her in my arms to reassure her. She laid her head on my shoulder and whispered, "Herman, I could say that if you want to leave me because we're childless, then the choice is yours. But you see, I don't believe I'm only a baby machine to you. I believe in us, that we are a couple who love each other in spite of everything."

And then, to our delight, in 1995 Nkhensani was born! Oh, the joy at the birth of our long-awaited little girl. At the time, I was travelling extensively, and my mother moved in with us to help Connie ease into motherhood. Although Connie had waited to be a mother for such a long time, she was inexperienced. And so, like every good granny, my mother wanted to make sure that Connie had the support she needed. My mother hadn't been able to be there through much of my own childhood, and her involvement in the lives of our children was her much-appreciated attempt to make up for that absence in my own life.

We were equally thrilled when our son, Rhulani, was born on 2 April 1996. Our family was now complete.

While Connie was attending with great zeal to her maternal duties in the years following 1995, I was taking care of our other child, which Connie refers to as "Herman's Baby". Black Like Me was a model child; her development was exemplary, and she rewarded Connie and me in so many ways – I enjoyed golf games with friends, and weekends away, and holidays with our friends and family, and we were able to travel extensively. By this time, we had already travelled to about sixty countries. I had broken the curse of the saying: people who are born in Hammanskraal grow up and die there.

When, as a young boy, I travelled on the train from

Hammanskraal to Pretoria or Johannesburg, I felt as if I was embarking upon an exciting adventure; later on, honeymooning in Durban and experiencing the ocean, and driving through the open spaces of the country to get there, had opened my eyes to the vastness of the country. But it was international travel that really exposed me to a world beyond, and to the diversity of cultures. Travel also taught me much by exposing me to the world's expectations of me; all I needed to do was open my eyes to the opportunities that existed and seize them.

Prior to 1994, travel among blacks was not merely financially difficult; getting a passport was such a logistical nightmare that few blacks bothered to apply. I had managed to obtain a passport fairly easily when I worked at SuperKurl because I needed to travel to Swaziland, Namibia, Lesotho and Botswana on business.

In those days, I especially enjoyed the run to Lesotho with Leon Thompson. Connie would wake up early and make me breakfast so that I could be on the road before dawn. In the coolest hours of the morning I drove to Leon's house so that we could leave at 5 am, before the morning rush-hour traffic snarled up the highways. Lesotho was a lucrative market for SuperKurl, and Leon and I would spend two or three days there promoting the products and writing up orders. It was during the five-hour drive to Lesotho, and at the inevitable border post wait, that I really got to know Leon. We would discuss business and, inevitably, the current affairs of the day. Leon was an astute executive, and although our trips were purposeful and deadline driven, the aim was to offer service, a good product, and get the maximum orders. During our conversations, I managed to gain an insight into the perceptions that black and white people had of each other, and how difficulties in understanding manifested themselves on both sides. I soon realised that our interaction wasn't so much a case of breaking down barriers as of realising the falseness and deceptiveness of stereotypes. Leon and I were in many ways equals, and our discussions revealed our commonality.

Shortly before I'd started Black Like Me in 1985, Connie and I took our first aeroplane flight and visited Cape Town, spending the week at the Cape Sun hotel. We felt as if we were in a parallel universe; hardly any black people were visible in the city streets, and one day as we were walking down St George's Mall, I turned to Connie and said, "Where the hell are the black people?" Fortunately, my sister Conny had told a nursing colleague, Adolphina Moleba, that we'd be visiting Cape Town, and Adolphina had arranged for a cousin of hers to show us around the city and its surrounding townships. Adolphina's cousin turned out to be none other than the recently banned Black Consciousness activist, Dr Mamphela Ramphele.

At that time, the apartheid government was forging ahead with its resettlement programmes, and it had built many houses in Khayelitsha. The people who were supposed to be relocated to Khayelitsha refused to leave the areas they were living in. There were many reasons why they didn't want to be resettled in this alien area, not the least of which was Khayelitsha's distance from business areas that offered jobs. I could sympathise with these people's sentiments because I myself was in the process of trying to find suitable premises for Black Like Me; in my own way, I knew how difficult it was living and working in areas that are off the beaten track.

From the mid-1980s to the late 1990s I seized any travelling opportunity that arose, and as a result I spent many days and weeks away from home, sometimes leaving Connie to keep an eye on the business. I worked hard to promote Black Like Me at whatever community opportunity arose, so as to keep the company in the public eye. We organised workshops in salons to train hairdressers in the appropriate use of our products, and we also ran hairdressing competitions and beauty competitions. As Black Like Me increased its market share, Connie and I could afford to take leisure trips overseas. Our first such trip was to Mauritius in 1986. We both found this beautiful island very different from South Africa. Mauritius was calm and harmonious – it was a relief and a joy to travel without having to look over our shoulders for someone waiting to accuse us of some racial offence.

Imagine me in 1986, in my mid-twenties, living in apartheid South Africa at a time when the state of emergency had just been declared, and all my leaders were exiled or in jail; here I was, operating a business from a modest factory in a remote South African township. And then, suddenly, I was off to America. My first international business trip was to New York. One of my friends and a regular customer, Goolam Kaka, was flying via New York to visit his sister in Canada, and we agreed to fly to New York together. When I went to the US embassy to apply for my visa I had to deal with bureaucrats who were uncertain about granting an American visa to a young black South African man. During the interview, I explained that I was in the beauty industry and that I was going to the States on a fact-finding mission. I had no business agenda, and I did not have a network of business contacts, but my air of confidence seemed to persuade them: the business visa was approved.

The flight stopped over in Ilha do Sal in the Cape Verde Islands, and during refuelling passengers were allowed to disembark and stretch their legs. We strolled to the airport building; it was midnight, but we decided to have a nightcap in the bar, and it was there that I met a fellow South African who told me he was a photographer for *The Sowetan*. We got chatting over a drink, and he mentioned that he'd be visiting a South African friend. "I'll be attending to some business in New York. We should get together one night for a meal."

It was fortunate that I had the worldly photographer as my

companion: when we landed at JFK airport, it was a complete culture shock – the vastness of it, the people and the chaos. The photographer's friend, Duma Ndlovu, was in exile at the time; he greeted all three of us warmly at the airport, and drove us to the Hilton Hotel on Sixth Avenue in Manhattan. After he'd seen to it that we were booked in, he said to Goolam and me, "Why don't you guys come to my apartment in Harlem? I'd love to introduce you to some exiles, I'm sure they'd love to hear some stories from home."

Duma was an excellent host, but the evening remains memorable because it was the first time I'd met fellow South Africans who were in exile. I found their thirst for information about South Africa quite humbling.

"Do you think apartheid will ever be dismantled?"

"What are the whites saying, what are they doing, about the situation?"

"Are there still protest meetings at Regina Mundi in Soweto?"

"Can there ever really be a peaceful solution for South Africa?"

"Hey, I miss eating apricots off the trees behind my granny's two-room in Dobsonville."

I felt moved by their longing for their homeland, their commitment to South Africa, the immense love they had for the country, and the hopes they had for its liberation. I lay awake a long time that night in my suite at the Hilton, my thoughts turning around the political situation in the country, and the people who desperately wanted the anti-apartheid struggle to succeed.

Duma was active in the arts, and over the next few days he took us to the Lincoln Centre and various sites of black activism in Harlem. One evening we dined together, sharing stories over delicious food and perhaps drinking one glass of wine too many. When the bill came, I insisted on paying. I suppose you could say that I felt I was in a better financial position to do so, after having seen Duma's modest Harlem home; my assumption was that he was the struggling exile and I was the successful businessman. Duma, however, refused to allow me to foot the bill.

At the time, there were a lot of government spies about, both black and white, who caused a lot of harm. Ruth First had been murdered in exile in Mocambique in 1982; though this had happened four years earlier, many exiles remained vigilant and suspicious of strangers. It is not surprising that Duma himself was apprehensive of this black guy – me – who was staying at the Hilton hotel.

"I was used to South African exiles who landed on my doorstep with empty pockets and grumbling bellies, and I was used to having to host them until they got used to New York and could stand on their own two feet," he later told me. "I couldn't help being suspicious when I first met you. I thought you might be on the Boers' payroll – until, that is, I read a newspaper article about you. It described how you manipulated the system and managed to develop a successful business outside the legal framework." Whenever Duma and I get together, we still reminisce about that first meeting in New York, and to this day we have a good laugh about it all.

At the time, after seeing the huge sacrifices made by Duma and the other exiles in their struggle for liberation in South Africa, I was forced to rethink the regret I'd felt as a young adult, the sense of bitter disappointment, that I had never managed to leave South Africa and join Umkhonto we Sizwe. I realised how fortunate I was to be building a successful business, which required my full attention, at a moment when the apartheid system was beginning to show signs of strain under international and local political pressure. How long it would to take for the government to yield to the pressure was not certain, but it was evident that the system was not sustainable. During my youth, none of us ever imagined that we would see the end of apartheid in our lifetime, but by the late 1980s a spark of hope lit our optimism. The dismantling of apartheid might take another ten or twenty years, but at last we sensed that the end of oppression was on the horizon.

In New York I had engaged with exiles who longed to return to the country of their birth, and yet they voiced their uncertainty about that hope ever becoming a reality. I'd felt an immense sympathy with them, living as they did with continual suspicion and uncertainty, having sacrificed family, friends and everything they knew and loved. Through this engagement with them, I no longer felt the desire to trade places with them, and I finally understood and accepted that my contribution to my country would not be that of someone who fought for change from outside her borders, but rather as an example of the kind of liberation that is achieved through personal independence. There are many kinds of freedom, but one certain path to freedom is taking responsibility for one's own life.

A month after I returned home from New York, South African Airways was prohibited from flying to the United States. This was part of the international boycott of the apartheid government, which gained momentum, so that every day brought increasing isolation.

Yet my own world was expanding. I had my business to attend to, and I continued to visit the United States, flying there two or three times a year on other international airlines to attend trade shows, particularly in Chicago, which hosted the annual American Health and Beauty Aids Institute trade shows for black haircare and beauty companies. It often happened that Connie, or one of my partners or staff members, accompanied me, and the excursions were always great learning experiences. These trips provided me with more than just product knowledge, the latest trends and business contacts – they also taught me a lot about people. I encountered impressive human beings who broke down many of the misconceptions I had developed about race and culture from my early life experiences. My exposure to open-minded people who had grown up without the shackles of hatred made me adamant in my refusal to tolerate any expression of racism in my presence. As a young adult, I had avoided contact with whites because I was still vulnerable, and I feared any threat to my dignity. But, fortunately, by the time I started interacting with white people I had matured. I knew who I was by then, and I knew that I was in control of my life – nobody could devalue me or my achievements without my permission.

Prior to meeting Johan Kriel at SuperKurl, I had interacted with white business people from large companies, selling their products on a commission basis, and during that time I had related to them at the same level; our business relationship was mutually valuable and beneficial. I met the CEOs of the companies I worked for because as their frontline, the commissioned sales person, I was a valuable asset to the company. I never allowed myself to be anyone's "boy". During these exchanges with the top management, I clearly saw that there was no reason for white managers to push around their black employees; that kind of behaviour does not make business sense. In my experience, most business managers strive to build good relationships with their staff members.

A positive attitude was one of the main ingredients in ensuring that I achieved success. By dwelling on negativity, one's mind becomes muddied; negativity obscures clarity of thought – and clear thinking is an essential element when it comes to making sound decisions. A positive attitude, on the other hand, opens the windows of the mind so that one is able to get a clear view of possibilities and opportunities.

In 1997, then-president Nelson Mandela hosted several international and local dignitaries on the occasion of his first return visit to Robben Island. Guests were flown to the island by helicopter, and Hilary Clinton and her daughter Chelsea, as well as actor Bill Cosby, were among the international contingent. Connie and I had also been invited, and we both felt the significance and poignancy of the occasion. We would finally be going to visit the notorious prison where Nelson Mandela had been incarcerated for eighteen years, before being transferred to Pollsmoor and later Victor Verster Prison on the mainland for the remaining nine years of his prison term.

I was immediately struck by the forbidding grey boulders surrounding the island harbour, and the shrieking of gulls in the solemn sky. The barbed wire and grey rock buildings conjured up the bleak atmosphere that the political prisoners had had to endure. We walked along the cell blocks, and eventually stood in front of a narrow fanlight window that ran the width of the corridor in Mandela's cellblock; the wind howled through the opening. At a deeply personal level, I imagined the suffering of the unfortunate men who were incarcerated on the island because they had refused the inhumane system that had stripped them of all choice and agency.

I felt as if I was walking in my sleep; it seemed unimaginable that I was standing in the great man's tiny cell – a cell that I had never dreamt of visiting in a democratic South Africa. The iron bedframe and coarse grey blanket were Mandela's only creature comforts during the long period he spent in that bleak island prison. This brought home to me the fact that Mandela's humanity did not come from having or not having; it was a quality that emanated from within.

The stone quarry where Mandela chopped limestone is a cheerless place; the limestone is blinding white in the harsh sunlight, and it caused agony and damage to the prisoners who were forced to chop it up into small pieces for road gravel. I took a photograph of Connie standing in the limestone cave where the prisoners had sought shelter from seething heat, dismal cold, piercing wind and driving rain. We were surprised at the large number of rabbits that hopped about the island and scurried into holes amid the scrubby fynbos.

Mandela and his fellow prisoners had succeeded in overcoming the misery of long-term incarceration by reading and debating issues among themselves, and many of them had studied through Unisa. In this way, he and his comrades had rescued themselves from being tainted by bitterness.

Books have been constant companions in my own life; it is through the solitary pursuit of reading that I have managed to educate myself and broaden the foundations of the inferior education that I received as a boy. By reading widely, I have tried to inform myself about the world and many of its remarkable people. Through books, I am constantly exposed to ideas that have resonated with me and helped me to consider and solve specific issues in my personal and business life. I believe, therefore, that libraries are very important resources for people with limited means. While interaction with people has taught me much, focused reading such as *Hearing Grasshoppers Jump: The Story of Raymond Ackerman*, is invaluable. This recent biography provides useful insights into the life and experiences of an entrepreneur with exceptional energy and vision. Books like this have always been useful aids that helped me to formulate ideas, create a business model for Black Like Me and ensure the company's future success.

Chapter 14

Bt 1997, Black Like Me had grown into a leading haircare company, but was not without its troubles along the way. There had been a major setback four years before. The company had entered a new phase of development on 17 November 1993 as a result of my determination to increase production. After consulting with my management board, we decided to put the company into 24-hour production. Additional staff members were hired to work the extra shift that was necessary to meet the revised production output. I held a meeting with the newly recruited staff members to confirm their duties and discuss the expectations and procedures of the company, and we were all filled with the sense that Black Like Me was on the brink of expansion.

I will never forget the events of that night. I returned home, and Connie and I enjoyed dinner together as we happily discussed the day's events. But our joy was short-lived. At 2 am the telephone rang. I picked it up, and the urgency in the security guard's voice broke through my foggy sleep.

"There is smoke coming out of the factory," he said.

"Are you sure it's a fire? Is the whole factory on fire, or just a part of it?" I asked disbelievingly.

The guard repeated, "There is a fire, sir. It is a big fire."

Connie and I dressed in silence, fumbling in the darkness, too stunned to even turn on the light.

As we drove, we asked each other inane questions; we could not – would not – believe that our dreams were going up in smoke.

The car slid along the muddy streets of Mabopane as we raced to see how bad the fire was and how much of the new facility had burnt down. Before leaving home, I had phoned the Ga-Rankuwa Fire Department, hoping that they would get there in time to prevent a complete catastrophe, but their phone was constantly engaged. I'd then phoned the Rosslyn Fire Department, and although they were quick to answer, they could not help.

"I'm sorry, the factory is out of our jurisdiction," they said.

I was furious, and I refused to be dismissed on the grounds of legalities – I had spent my life finding ways around official protocol. On the way to the factory, I took a slight detour, hoping that a personal approach would soften their response, hoping that when they saw our desperation they would relent and help us. I pulled into the Rosslyn Fire Station, rushed inside, and explained that the company had just taken delivery of packaging material that would melt like wax if we did not stop the fire, it soon became clear that they were not going to go out of their way to prevent the destruction of our factory.

We felt helpless and angry as we got back into the car and drove on. Through the dawn sky, we saw the smoke; in a couple of devastating minutes we watched as bright flames devoured the factory. The premises were surrounded by curious spectators, and the flames lit their faces; the blazing spectacle stunned us all into silence. As the clock crept towards 6 am, the newly appointed and long-standing staff members started to arrive. The questions on their faces were easy to read.

"What happened?"

"How did the fire start?"

And the most urgent question of all: "What will happen to our jobs?"

Through it all, I knew that I had to be strong for Connie and my employees, and I remember turning to my old friend, Louis.

"This fire is a challenge, but we're going to rise above it. I won't allow it to ruin us," I said.

I reassured everybody that Black Like Me had not died in that fire, that we would rise out of the ashes. These were encouraging words that I am not entirely sure I felt at the time, but I knew that the only way out was forward. As the owner of the company it was my duty to guide my employees through that dark period.

In the aftermath of the fire, there were nasty rumours. These were fanned by people who insisted that the fire was not an act of God, but arson. It was hard to ignore these rumours that jealous people were spreading to try to destroy me, but this was not my first experience of this kind of rumour-mongering. A similar thing had happened in the early days of Black Like Me, when I was making enough money to be able to help other people get their businesses started.

My brother Pobane was one of those who came to me for assistance.

"I've got a chance to become a partner in a business," he said to me one day with a smile of anticipation. "Some of my friends have won a contract to hang curtains and fit carpets. But they are stuck, Herman, they need money. They haven't got proper transport for the materials. We need a bakkie, my brother."

Pobane and I visited some motor dealerships and we test-drove a few bakkies. When Pobane felt that he had found a vehicle that suited the business's purposes, I bought it for him. I hoped that his new business venture would at last enable him to provide for his young family.

The first of the ugly rumours about Black Like Me began when Pobane died in the accident. In the customary way, we held a vigil the night before the funeral, and it was there that vicious rumours circulated.

"They did it – Herman and his mother. Mrs Mashaba."

"It was a witchdoctor's muti that caused the accident."

"E-e, it was not an accident. No, man. Pobane was killed. He was sacrificed so that they will become richer."

The vile suggestions that my mother and I had arranged

my brother's death so that Black Like Me could flourish were based on foolish cultural beliefs that still prevail in certain communities.

As a Christian, I have never subscribed to these kinds of notion, which I regard as negative, limiting and destructive. Nevertheless, the accusation that I had in some way been responsible for Pobane's death was extremely upsetting to my family and to me in particular. It was inconceivable to me that some people actually believed that I had engaged in murder for the benefit of my business. Or were they just fabricating rumours out of jealousy, trying to ruin my reputation? Whatever their motive, I made it clear that business success has nothing to do with muti or ancestral spirits; people need to focus on their own living spirit to be successful.

After the fire, I was once again faced with rumours fuelled by people's jealousy of my success. And though I was annoyed by it all, I did have my own suspicions about a certain ex-employee. So, armed with the necessary evidence, I went to the police and asked them to investigate the person whom I suspected was involved in the fire.

I believed that the fire was a result of economic jealousy, but that the perpetrator was sharp enough to take advantage of the extreme crime and violence in the townships at the time, knowing that the overtaxed police did not have sufficient resources to devote attention to a suspected arson attack. In frustration, I consulted the company's lawyers and we offered a substantial reward, hoping that someone would come forward with information. We never received any leads, though. For some inexplicable reason the case was never investigated, and to this day it lies gathering dust in a police basement somewhere. There is no point in dwelling on the setbacks in life, and so I moved on, turning my attention instead to delivering on my promise to rebuild the company.

Shortly before the Black Like Me fire, the shopping mall

belonging to my ex-partner, Walter Dube, burnt down. At the time, I owned a butchery in the mall, which my cousin, Benny Sebopa, ran. When Walter lodged his claim with the insurance company, he got a nasty shock – the insurance company had declared bankruptcy. Outraged, Walter phoned me.

"Herman, you should change Black Like Me's insurance company. You'd better do it right now," he said.

"What are you talking about?" I said.

"Black Like Me is insured by the company I was insured with, and it won't pay out," he said.

As it turned out, I would receive no compensation for damage to the butchery either. But, in the meantime, I acted on Walter's advice and immediately changed to a different company.

I made the change just in time. After the fire that destroyed Black Like Me, I lodged a claim for fire damage, but after the insurance company's investigation they advised that they would only pay out for damage to the building and not for its contents. This was a bad blow, as prior to the fire Black Like Me was at the height of its production, its machinery cache was extensive, and so was its stock of product and packaging materials. Without the insurance money to cover the replacement of these costly items, Black Like Me was in a financial predicament. I could not afford the time that a dispute with the insurance company would have demanded of me, and so I had no alternative but to fund the losses with my personal capital.

After Connie and I had moved to Heatherdale, we had been only mildly concerned with our safety, but subsequent to the fire, we began to have other thoughts.

"Herman, if the rumours of arson are true, maybe they'll attack this house next. They could come here and try to kill you. Both our lives could be in danger," Connie said to me a few days after the fire. "I can't live with the stress of fearing for our lives; you have to do something," she said.

It was clear to me that Connie had been traumatised by the

fire, and I fully understood her concerns about our safety. After this, I employed two personal bodyguards. The men I hired were ex-British Special Forces servicemen, and their services were tagged at the exorbitantly high monthly fee of R30 000. Having bodyguards was not only expensive, it was also a strange experience, and after a few months I began to find the procedures more suffocating than reassuring. So I decided I would take my chances with anyone who wanted to challenge me.

Our first task after the fire was finding new premises. I spent a couple of days looking at sites with an agent in Pretoria, but we couldn't afford the time it would take to build a new factory. In any case, we were now living under a new dispensation and I was no longer bound by restrictive group areas laws – I could establish a factory anywhere I liked. So, instead of looking for land I inspected existing factories, and after about ten days I found suitable premises in Midrand. It was not all plain sailing, though. In spite of the company's impressive financial growth, banks were still reluctant to give black businesses loans, so, without a loan or an insurance payout, I personally had to fund the re-establishment of Black Like Me.

Louis was a tremendous support to me during this time. He had joined Black Like Me in 1992, first as a salesman. He was really good at his job, and he was soon promoted to sales manager. I gave Louis a personal cheque to pay for the factory, which he delivered to the transferring attorneys. The location of the new factory meant a time-consuming commute from Pretoria, but I had no alternative.

The specialised machinery that we had amassed over the years could not be replaced overnight, and as I tackled the mammoth task ahead of us, it felt as though I was teaching Black Like Me to walk again. The situation forced us to go back to basics, and the company had to make some serious decisions.

Strong businesses are built by strong people, and the company employees were instrumental in rebuilding Black Like Me. Two weeks after the fire we started operating in the Midrand factory, but we could not possibly take up from where we had left off; it was not just a case of business as usual. Without the necessary machinery, we did not have the capacity to produce a full complement of Black Like Me products. So we decided to chart a strategy that was feasible, without continually looking back over our shoulders at what production had been "before the fire".

One of the company's most dedicated employees was Meshack Mahlangu, affectionately known as Madonsi; he was the factory manager, and he took charge of "Mission Recovery". He organised, strategised and worked at maximum capacity to ensure that we met our targets and commitments. I have rarely experienced such dedication from an employee. While the staff gave their all to our recovery plan, we were logistically frustrated. Suppliers with standing orders to deliver chemicals and packaging had to be contacted and advised of our changed circumstances. We had to inform them where to deliver, or what supplies were no longer required; this huge task demanded co-ordination and co-operation from all the parties involved, and the Black Like Me staff proved their mettle.

At the time of the fire, Black Like Me had a range of 120 products, but we were no longer able to produce all of them. We took the decision to produce only limited lines that could be manufactured with the machinery that we were able to buy at that point. Some of these lines, in particular Step 1, which was a big seller at the time, enjoyed excellent margins and was easy to manufacture. Using a few 1 000-litre drums and a single stirrer, we went back into production; once again, our bottles had to be filled manually. However, this time I was not able to involve myself in the manufacturing process; I had to get out to customers and explain our situation and ensure that they were aware of our reduced capabilities. The production line was extended to its limit, but throughout this difficult time, the staff were unswerving in their support.

Before the fire, Black Like Me had enjoyed a prominent position in the market, but afterwards our sales plummeted. November and December were traditionally the best trading months of the year, but with only a single product in the market, our turnover plunged. Consumer demand was still enormous, but salons were forced to look to our competitors to satisfy their needs. Inevitably, our turnover decreased dramatically. But it was not only the fire that crippled the company; the post-1994 election saw an unprecedented increase in crime, and Black Like Me did not escape unscathed. The immediate effect of the crime wave was on our staff; three were hijacked while doing company deliveries, including Louis. Informal township salons that had no – or very limited – security were soft targets, and theft had a ripple effect that eventually reached Black Like Me. Our company policy had been to sell products to salon owners on credit, but because they were mostly uninsured, they were unable to pay their suppliers for stock that had been stolen. In the Black Like Me boardroom management discussed this problem at length, but we were eventually forced to take the tough decision not to extend credit. As a result, we found ourselves in a catch-22 situation: we could not afford to extend credit, and some customers could not buy without terms of credit. At times, it felt as if the company was taking one step forward and two steps back.

The original hopes I'd had of expanding Black Like Me were shelved. The company was only just hanging on to its reduced market share – and so we were forced to focus on survival rather than expansion.

After 1994, with the new ANC government in power, attempts were made to address racial disparities in business advancement. Whites had enjoyed the monopoly in business, and the new government was eager to show its commitment to change. Black Economic Empowerment (BEE) became the buzzword, and my peers and friends were approaching me with business ideas to take advantage of the situation. But no matter how frustrated I was with our company's slow creep back to its former dominant position in the haircare industry, I had little inclination to investigate BEE.

I was constantly being approached by companies to sell Black Like Me and to retain a BEE position within the company, but I was not at all interested in doing so. To be honest, I felt insulted at times when I watched as some of my peers allowed themselves to be wooed by corporates, only to end up occupying the corner office with nothing to keep them busy other than the view from their office window. I have always had a strong work ethic and I had no inclination to be a ja-broer on a corporate board; if I were ever to decide to join the BEE bandwagon, I'd make sure I was the person driving it, and not one of the people reclining on the back of the vehicle.

So I rejected the offers I received and concentrated on Black Like Me, gradually building it up again. It took eighteen painstaking months for the company to get back on its feet, and by the end of 1994 our limited production line had grown by about 40%. On average, four 18-metre shipping containers were being delivered to distributors daily, and the staff complement had grown to 160. Black Like Me had finally emerged from the ashes.

With the company's local production stabilised, I had to look ahead and mark the next target on the board. Convinced that our future lay in going global, I started to investigate foreign markets and tried to marshal my ideas into a coherent strategy. Initially we established distribution contracts in Zambia, Malawi and the DRC, and also in Lesotho, Namibia and Swaziland, and then Louis and I visited Kenya and Zimbabwe to forge links with suppliers there.

It was only by being in charge of its destiny that I could lead Black Like Me in the direction I wanted. I saw no benefit in taking on a partner who would merely be retracing my footsteps – and I was certainly not prepared to follow anyone else's trail.

Chapter 15

By 1996, the euphoria that had followed in the wake of the elections was over. The rest of the world recognised the genuine reforms that the new government was undertaking, and the United Nations lifted the trade embargo against South Africa. The government forged ahead with foreign trade deals, specifically with India and China, but, more importantly for Black Like Me, locally it was fast-tracking black empowerment.

In order to comply with BEE legislation that was in the process of being ratified, many white buyers were making offers to buy black-owned companies in various configurations; a black face would entitle the buyer to BEE status. I was not interested in any of this: I did not even bother to analyse the legislation. Black Like Me was successful in its own right, and the companies that were approaching me needed me more than I needed them. I stuck firm to my principles, refusing to entertain any of these bids.

In just two years, Black Like Me had increased turnover to a level I was happy with. Diplomatic ties with countries further afield, such as Ghana, Mali and Senegal, had been established, opening up even more trade with countries that offered lucrative markets for our products. But our forays into Africa were hampered by unpaid debts as well as the usual problems with the clearance of goods at ports of entry; communication was also a problem, and I began to view these new markets with scepticism.

It serves no purpose to harp on the inequalities of the past, yet I must admit that the limits in my education had resulted in my relying largely on gut feel in the running of my company. I knew that Black Like Me needed to expand internationally, but at the same time it needed the benefit of mature business experience. So, when Colgate-Palmolive approached me eventually, I looked at the offer coolly and decided to give it due consideration. That company's penetration into international markets was well established, and it had a body of corporate expertise that would fill the gaps in my style of management. Expanding Black Like Me on a continental scale required the enormous capital reserves of a company such as Colgate-Palmolive, whose credibility would be an asset in helping to reach the level of success I'd envisaged.

Networking with managers in the corporate world had given me access to advisers, and I had benefited greatly from their experience and advice. Shortly before the Colgate-Palmolive offer, I was having a conversation with my friend and business colleague, Rod Fehrsen, who was with the PG group – South Africa's oldest and largest plate glass manufacturer.

"I need a good tax adviser," I mentioned.

"I've got just the man for you – Shane Ferguson," was his instant reply.

Our first meeting was scheduled for an hour, and Shane ended up staying three, I'd immediately felt at ease with his unassuming manner. Shane was late for our second meeting and every subsequent meeting, and I realised that this was to become a pattern. It soon became apparent that Shane likes to focus on the matter at hand and to resolve issues there and then, before moving on to the next client. Waiting for Shane to show up for a meeting became the norm rather than the exception.

At one of these meetings, I said to him, "Listen, I've had two offers for my business – one from Carsons Holdings. And now there's also one from Colgate-Palmolive." I explained the situation. "Carsons want to buy the entire company, but this Colgate deal allows me to retain a working position in it."

Shane nodded, and I went on. "The Colgate deal is more to my benefit. I'd be able to realise my ambitions for Black Like Me – and I'll also retain a 25% share in it."

"Yes, the Colgate deal sounds good, Herman. Knowing what I do of you, it'll suit you better. You'll still be active in the company, and still have some control," Shane said.

I was relieved to hear him say this, and said, "Do you think you could help me negotiate a deal with Colgate-Palmolive?"

He was eager to assist me to conclude a deal with Colgate, even though it would be an awkward situation; I had been negotiating with Carsons, and they had already made a media announcement about the deal they were hoping to conclude. I provided Shane with details, which he tackled immediately and energetically.

After much careful discussion of the Colgate offer with Shane and my advisers, I felt satisfied that I had a viable deal. I set down very specific conditions for the buy-out. I did not want to lose control of the company; I would not consider any relationship where I'd become an overpaid employee gathering dust in a corner office; and I wanted a clear vision of the growth and expansion that Colgate-Palmolive had in mind for Black Like Me.

From the preliminary negotiations with Colgate-Palmolive's David Conn, it was clear that we shared the same aspirations for the merger.

"The Colgate-Palmolive/Black Like Me partnership should be a win-win situation for both companies," Conn said as we shook hands on the deal. Colgate had recognised the vast potential of the ethnic haircare market, but their efforts to penetrate it had been unsuccessful. Black Like Me had expert product knowledge and extensive experience of the market, but we did not have the well-established distribution network and the technical and marketing resources that Colgate-Palmolive enjoyed. We indeed had much to offer each other.

When the agreement was finally drawn up, it was the size of the Bible. Colgate had lawyers from the United States, Canada and South Africa working on the draft agreement, but Black Like Me only had just Shane looking after its interests. We sat down to sign the agreement, but it took till 4 am to conclude the negotiations.

During post-election South Africa, the rail transport system underwent changes, and Black Like Me could no longer rely on its services. When awarding contracts, I had, where possible, always used a black contractor – and I make no apologies for this. But many of these distributors were erratic in their delivery because they lacked a disciplined, professional business ethic. Building a brand depends on reliability and consistency, and because of the poor supply-chain distribution, Black Like Me was not able to maintain the requisite consistency of supply to other African states.

In addition to these logistical problems, crime was rampant. Informal retailers were a high risk to insurers and as a result salon owners were unable to secure insurance against losses. So, whenever they were burgled or burnt down, it was Black Like Me that ultimately bore the risk. We had implemented a credit scheme that proved ineffective, and it became necessary to review our customer base and reconsider whether we wanted to continue with distribution to informal traders or whether we wanted to concentrate solely on national supermarket and trade wholesaler distribution.

The situation was further complicated by strong competition from other beauty and haircare companies – especially Carson Holdings and Procter & Gamble. Increased pressure from competing products forced Black Like Me to up its game. This meant reformulating products, but the research and development involved was costly and time consuming, even though we had a team of four chemists working under Dan Pooe. I hoped that Colgate's technical resources would help us cut down on the research and development phase. Another issue was packaging. Our international competitors had invested a lot of money in this, thus forcing Black Like Me to upgrade its packaging if we were to compete on the shelves.

Bearing all this in mind, Black Like Me married Colgate-Palmolive on 1 July 1997. It felt rather as if I was letting go of my first "child", but I had not realised that selling 75% of our company to Colgate would also be an emotional experience for Connie. However, sentiment has never been a feature of my business dealings, whose primary focus has always been profit. Colgate's motivation for wanting to buy the company resonated with me: the deal made good business sense.

All marriages have their settling-in period as partners get to know each other, and the merger between Colgate and Black Like Me was no different. However, both companies sought to minimise the uncertainty that the merger presented to the Black Like Me staff, so we appointed a consultancy company to work with the staff, explaining the reason for the merger – increased production and market penetration – and also to clarify the benefits of increased staff training and development. My request to retain my position in Black Like Me was honoured, and I was appointed Managing Director as I knew the industry inside out – Colgate also realised that I would not be content to sit on the sidelines while they took over the reins.

In spite of the buy-out, our market share continued to slide. Yet I went against my better judgement, ignoring my gut feeling that things were not going according to plan. I persevered, patiently allowing alien systems and controls to be implemented. But soon the situation became all too apparent, and after three years, I could no longer continue ignoring it. Finally, acknowledging my frustration, I said to Connie, "It's not working. There's not the synergy that either side expected. And I can't, in good conscience, just stand by and watch as Black Like Me slides into obscurity." Then I phoned Shane Ferguson.

"Shane, this marriage is over, you need to negotiate a divorce," I said.

It was one of the lowest ebbs of my life.

I had established Black Like Me on the whiff of an oil rag, built it into a multi-million-rand corporation, watched as it burned to the ground, and then rebuilt it again – I was not going to watch another meltdown. This time, there seemed no way that I could resuscitate Black Like Me.

I had hoped that Colgate's buy-out would be the boost that Black Like Me needed, but I realised that if they couldn't help me take the company to the heights I'd hoped for, then it was time to finally let go of the reins. I mandated Shane to negotiate with Colgate-Palmolive for the buy-out of my remaining 25% of Black Like Me shares. Negotiations went on for six months, and my plans were not resolved in quite the way I expected. Then Shane came to see me and said, "How would you like to buy your baby back?" Instead of Colgate-Palmolive buying my shares, they offered me the opportunity to buy back all my Black Like Me shares.

This was a completely unforeseen development. I had sold 75% of the company for a large sum of money.

"Where the hell will I get the money to buy it back?" I said to Connie in despair. "I have no idea what price tag Colgate will attach to the shares. I don't know if I've got enough capital to buy it all back – in fact, I don't even know if I want to buy it back."

I'd reached a stage where I felt I no longer had anything to prove. I had built a successful and respected business; there were offers of BEE deals everywhere I turned; and I had a beautiful young family – Connie, Nkhensani and Rhulani – who'd have welcomed my undivided attention. Connie said as much when she reminded me, "Herman, we can live comfortably for the rest of our lives, even if you don't ever work another day."

I was faced with a dilemma. My own security and comfort

were irrelevant concerns, but I did have to consider the staff at Black Like Me; they had been with me on all the ups and downs of the company's roller-coaster ride. Also, there were all the community projects that Black Like Me sponsored and supported. I soon realised that I wasn't ready to let it all go. And, most of all, I wanted to be in charge of my own business again.

Through some difficult negotiations, Shane and I managed to buy back the 75% share for less than Colgate had paid. It was a significant coup, and it re-energised me. On 1 August 1999 Black Like Me was mine again – I was determined that nothing would hold me back from returning the company to its former position in the beauty industry.

Once again, Shane Ferguson had brokered a good deal for me, so I gave him shares in the company. Although Shane and I are business partners first, we are also friends. His finest quality is his fairness in all his dealings. Since our first meeting, Shane has served as my adviser in almost every business transaction that I have undertaken – his lack of guile and honest approach to business have helped to ensure sustainable business transactions, and have also prevented corporate headaches that may have occurred. He is a true business professional who knows how to structure a deal and how to get funding; he also has an excellent network, and an innate ability to add value to business transactions. I have watched Shane get married, and Connie and I have also celebrated the birth of his two lovely daughters, our families becoming close friends.

Although we operate independently, Shane is a shareholder in some of my businesses; he also does most of my legal and corporate work. If I could learn to enjoy fishing or Shane could learn to enjoy golf, we'd spend a lot more time together.

The dawn of the millennium heralded the beginning of a new era for Black Like Me. It had taken three years for corporate

rigidity to near-strangle the flexible and organic company I had
built up over fifteen years or so. "I won't allow it happen again,"
I said to Shane. "I must think very, very carefully about the next
step I take."

While I didn't want to sell Black Like Me, I realised that there
would be other business opportunities, and that I needed
to elevate my presence and profile in the corporate world. I
became more accommodating of the media, who wanted to
profile me as a business success; it would have been selfish and
counter-productive to continue to safeguard Herman Mashaba,
the man, from media attention. I was regularly asked to deliver
motivational lectures to various organisations that sought to
elevate an emerging black management, and who regarded the
success achieved by Black Like Me as a positive model. New
managers needed to see black success stories.

With this in mind, I put myself at the forefront of reforming
Black Like Me. Buying back the company had used up almost
all my financial reserves, and for a while we operated on a
hand-to-mouth basis. But by getting back to basics, re-hiring
key staff, and re-establishing the company's focus, we were
able to achieve phenomenal sales in 2001, and accelerated
earnings a year later – realising an astonishing 40% growth.
Black Like Me had expanded its product range, modernised
the packaging, and included French wording on products so
that they could compete on shelves against our competitors in
Francophone Africa. I employed an export manager to attend
to communication with port authorities and to focus on our
business networks in Ethiopia, Cameroon, Mauritius, Zambia
and Kenya. We concentrated on revitalising our waning support
in Botswana, and Louis led the re-launch there by holding a
promotion for Black Like Me as well as our Perfect Choice and
Special Solutions brands. Perfect Choice was aimed at creating
a black urban professional identity, and Special Solutions was
formulated to appeal to trend-conscious teenagers – a market

we hadn't considered up to then. We also sponsored the "Face of Africa" pageant.

In spite of its growth, Black Like Me had managed to acquire only 10% of the South African haircare market, which was worth about R600 million at the time. But from previous experience I knew that we also had to look ahead to the next logical step – international penetration.

The previous year, during a British trade visit to South Africa, I'd met a representative of haircare company Renbow International. But in spite of my keenness to co-operate with them, it took me a full two years to study the UK market and formulate a penetration strategy. The UK black haircare business model was quite different from the South African one. With 40 million people, the South African market was valued at R800 million, while the UK market consisted of a mere 3 million people, with an astonishing market value of about R740 million. The British black hair-care market was worth a lot, and I wanted Black Like Me to have a shot at securing a share of it. I was convinced that we had a superior product, so I took a gamble and threw the Black Like Me dice onto the board, clearly announcing its presence in the game.

I approached Renbow, and on 17 April 2002 Black Like Me was launched in London. We entered into a joint venture by which Renbow undertook the UK distribution of our product. During the early days of Black Like Me, Walter Dube used to joke about my extravagant marketing exercises – and now, inspired by my deal with Renbow, I decided to go really big. With the UK launch pending, I approached the Department of Trade and Industry and requested the use of South Africa House on Trafalgar Square for the British launch of Black Like Me. It was a bit of a bold move, so I was not really surprised when an official from the department phoned and asked me to explain. He politely asked, "What is your reason for wanting to host the launch at South Africa House?"

I explained that I was competing in an international arena against multinational companies, and that it would be good for South Africa to demonstrate that they too had credible heavyweights in industry. This satisfied the official, and soon we were making plans for the launch. Her Excellency Ms Lindiwe Mabuza was the High Commissioner at the time, and she graciously welcomed us at the embassy. It was a poignant moment for me as I stood outside South Africa House to welcome guests at the very spot where so many South African activists had toyi-toyi'd against the apartheid regime. It was a glittering occasion attended by the elite of London's black hairdressing community, trade diplomats and expats; Jean Pascal Brunas of Renbow addressed the gathering as we sipped champagne under crystal chandeliers.

The Black Like Me experience was rather like being in a boxing ring. I had entered as a lightweight, seeing my fair share of knocks to the ground. I had bloodied my nose and been up against the ropes more times than I cared to remember, but like any professional fighter, I stood up each time and took on the next challenger. Each new contender taught me a few more techniques, and I was able to dodge the jabs that come out of nowhere. The Colgate-Palmolive venture taught me that the large corporate structure is not the only viable model in a vibrant capitalist economy such as ours. Big corporate companies are essential, but emerging small-to-medium businesses are the lifeblood of sustained growth in a developing country. South Africa makes it easy for entrepreneurs to get started. There is an enormous untapped labour market, materials are cheap in comparison with many western markets, and we have excellent business infrastructure in terms of access to commercial properties for trade purposes – and, most importantly, we have accessible and robust financial services, as well as advanced telecommunications that facilitate easy communication.

Chapter 16

The new century ushered in a thrilling decade for South African business. Black Economic Empowerment saturated parliamentary debates and almost daily the phrase screamed out from newspaper posters at traffic-weary motorists. Connie and I rarely attended a business function without someone asking, "So, Herman, what do you and Connie think – who will BEE benefit? Will it help the disadvantaged, or will it make the elite even richer?" TV debates raged around the possibility of white businesspeople taking advantage of BEE opportunities by hiding behind black faces. I shared some of these reservations and concerns, but I also felt a growing interest in and sense of excitement at what BEE might achieve.

I'd had reservations about the strategy for some time, but by now I was beginning to feel curious as to what BEE might really mean for South Africa. Black South Africans had been severely disadvantaged under apartheid, as I knew from experience. My own family had lived in a "homeland", where the pass system forced them to work in areas with very few employment prospects, and transport services were severely limited. Though the entrepreneurial spirit has long been active, apartheid punished black entrepreneurs for their endeavours. Not even Walter Dube had escaped the pettiness of apartheid laws. As a young entrepreneur who'd grown his first meagre earnings into a thriving shebeen, he became the target of jealous local officials, who shut him down. Of course, Walter bounced back, but not everyone had Walter's resilience.

By 2000, it was apparent that the government had plans to create an enabling environment for black entrepreneurs, but no one was sure what changes would be brought about, and how these would be implemented. The talk at the time was that BEE was a form of affirmative action that created opportunities for returning exiles as well as struggle activists and their families. Watching some of these men and women make big money very quickly, I felt that Black Like Me had taken a long, long road to success when there was a shortcut; suddenly, the company's success felt like a bit of an anti-climax. I had built up a company without the help of banks or government. I had always been my own boss. Yet, still, I found myself wondering whether there might be an opportunity for an entrepreneur like me to participate in BEE. But would I have to be subservient to a corporation's rules? Would I merely be a black front for a white company? Not likely. But I could not ignore the persistent niggle that perhaps somewhere there was a place for me in a BEE company.

Richard Maponya and I were among those who had been active in the black entrepreneurial space for many years. But suddenly new names began to emerge – Patrice Motsepe, Tokyo Sexwale and others who, until then, were relatively unknown in the business world. Critics suggested at the time that many BEE deals were being concluded by an emergent black capitalist class that did not have the necessary cohesion to articulate its vision with confidence. This emergent group was, furthermore, criticised for its nationalist mindset: having emerged from the classless anti-apartheid struggle, they were said to lack class consciousness. They were criticised for being politically correct, for their apparently unconscious acceptance of the notion that it was wrong to accumulate wealth. Of course, there was irony in all this, but it nevertheless depressed me that the group adhered to such a notion: it fundamentally contradicted my own unapologetic support of capitalism. For many of the struggle generation, the accumulation of wealth was equated with greed, arrogance and the abuse of power. Indeed, such vices do exist. But to me it seemed counter-productive to indulge this mode of thinking. We need to be genuine champions of transforming our economy; if we are to establish a truly national business culture, the economy must be a true reflection of our national composition.

I believed strongly in bringing about meaningful reform, and so I had been active in the first democratic elections. Black Like Me was a funder of the Voter Education Forum run by Dr David Molapo, his wife Mmamiki, and Abner Mariri from the I Can Foundation. During my involvement in the Forum in 1994, I was able to hear the full range of political candidates – the Democratic Party, the ANC, the NNP, all of them. I listened as they all made big promises to the electorate, and it soon became clear that the one promise they all had in common was "Jobs for All". I was sceptical; as an employer, I doubted whether any of the politicians knew who would provide the large-scale jobs they were promising. Business is about making money; it is not about creating jobs.

It is easy to make election promises, as politicians do all the time: "Vote for Jobs"; "Vote for Houses."

When the voting public make their marks on the ballot paper, they do so because they expect delivery on electoral promises. In the same way that the election promises of jobs perplexed me, I was equally puzzled about the relationship between job creation and BEE. Was it all just election rhetoric? Yet I pricked up my ears: if the government's intention was to create jobs, it had to be looking at local businesses to provide those jobs, and as a business owner I needed to know how this might affect me. I couldn't understand how the government believed they could simply create jobs, because in my mind a business is created to satisfy a demand for products and services, and to make profits for the owner. As such, jobs are a by-product.

In those early days, the government's BEE programmes seemed to turn the spotlight on ownership – increasing black participation in ownership. But as its vision expanded, the government brought in further elements to encourage black empowerment. Among these were corporate social investment (the responsibilities of business towards civil society); enterprise development (financial or non-financial contributions to accelerate the development of a beneficiary); and employment equity (ensuring equitable representation in all levels of the workforce by previously disadvantaged employees). These elements all shifted the focus to broad-based ownership and the wider empowerment responsibilities of a company. I finally got it: BEE wasn't only about new job creation, but rather about restructuring existing business models to accommodate members of a previously disadvantaged workforce – employees who couldn't get the job of their choice due to discrimination, whether this be on the basis of gender or race or lack of educational qualifications.

By now I had been in the cosmetics industry for twenty years, and the time had come to move on; perhaps there was a way for me to venture into new pastures to create a sustainable business. While speaking to the people in my network, I discovered that I had missed out on some excellent opportunities. Among those who had taken early advantage of the situation was Patrice Motsepe, a sharp attorney who had jumped into BEE and cleverly secured options on disused mineshafts, which he then reopened. Motsepe made a fortune, and today he is a billionaire on the Forbes list. I decided to throw my earlier qualms and caution to the winds, but by then many BEE opportunities had already been seized. One evening, Connie and I were having a long discussion about the situation, and I eventually said to her, "I'd better start getting familiar with exactly what BEE entails, because with or without me, BEE is a reality in South Africa." Connie agreed, and I decided to move into the next phase of my business career.

I did intensive research into BEE, and was surprised to discover that many deals that had been brokered were in fact reallocation deals in which shares were merely allocated to previously disadvantaged employees. Despite there being an obvious material benefit to shareholders, the share allocation model was a handout that in no way empowered the staff who benefited from it – the maintenance manager was still the maintenance manager, and the tea maker was still the tea maker. As an entrepreneur, I believed that share allocation was short-sighted; it was nothing more than a salve to corporate consciences. While I appreciated the social philosophy behind the model and the need for redress, I also realised that this BEE model was merely shuffling things around, it was not developing entrepreneurs. The truth is, South Africa needs entrepreneurship, which benefits the economy by providing sustainable economic growth.

I decided that if I was going to be a BEE participant, I would have to locate suitable business vehicles that would allow me to proceed in the business arena with integrity. There was some irony, of course, in accepting the benefits of my "previously disadvantaged status", for I had succeeded in spite of apartheid disadvantages. I needed to fuse the BEE controls with my personal business ethics.

There are many concerns about BEE, but I believe that the government was absolutely right in enforcing it. However, without the support of strong business leaders, BEE cannot hope to develop an entrepreneurial spirit; business leaders must therefore incentivise entrepreneurs by encouraging, supporting and coaching them in good business practice. While many black South Africans are willing to create jobs, they have not acquired the necessary business skills to sustain their businesses; it is precisely this lack of business acumen that perpetuates their disadvantaged status. While many will argue that it is impossible to teach entrepreneurship, I believe that it is vital that educational institutions and businesses teach entrepreneurial skills – self-motivational skills, time-management skills, financial skills, administrative skills, and sales and marketing skills – all of which can and need to be taught, not only to students, but also to employees. Failure to equip our workforce with these important entrepreneurial skills will frustrate the entrepreneurial spirit of the country.

When I turned to investigating BEE opportunities, I realised that whatever I chose to become involved in would require a large financial investment. I needed funding, so I consulted with other business executives and discussed my intentions with Shane Ferguson. Having done so, I made a media announcement that I intended to start a BEE investment company.

With Connie ably managing Black Like Me, I was able to devote all my time to establishing a new company. The first step was to investigate possible partners in order to establish a BEE investment company. The legislation insisted that BEE companies broaden their ownership. This was a response to criticism that BEE had benefited only a few black entrepreneurs – the Black Diamonds, as successful black people have come to be known. The new legislation wanted to see empowerment of black ownership on a broad base – including both men and women, and able-bodied as well as those who are physically challenged. In response to this technical requirement, I had to consider how broadly I would develop ownership. Also, I knew that I would be competing against business owners who had a political background.

I therefore phoned my friend, Ronnie Mamoepa, who was at the time spokesperson for the Department of Foreign Affairs. I explained my situation and ended by saying, "Ronnie, I'm moving into the BEE space and I need to put together the right type of profile."

Ronnie suggested a couple of names and I checked them against the people I had in mind; soon I'd put together a group I thought might be interested. I approached Max Sisulu, who held a senior position in the ANC at the time, though he wasn't in government. Then I approached Tommy Makgatho, who ran a string of supermarkets in Qwa-Qwa. Tommy was a Black Like Me distributor in the Free State, but also a friend who had travelled all over the world with me and my family in the early 1990s.

"Tommy, I'm giving up shampoo and going into BEE – come and join me," I said when I called him.

"Hey, what do I know about BEE? No, I'm not keen to go into anything right now – but maybe I'll consider it when I know a bit more about it," he said.

I continued canvassing, and eventually I had a group that included Max Sisulu, Ronnie Mamoepa, Jerry Majatladi, Sipho Madlopha, Thebi Moja, Puseletso Ramoipone, Jacqueline Mufamadi and Jane Phiri – people I hoped would give me the BEE profile that was needed by the new legislation. Not long afterwards, Leswikeng Mineral & Energy (Pty) Ltd was born.

The problem was finding the first vehicle – the starter-pack, if you will – to launch the investment company. This took a while, but eventually Shane Ferguson came up with some useful information: "Samancor own the Mogale Alloys smelter in Krugersdorp, which they've mothballed because the ferrochrome industry has fallen into a slump." He said, "A whole lot of white senior management at Samancor have been retrenched from the closed facility. But there's this ex-employee, Johan Oosthuizen, who says that the closure of the plant could be an opportunity for them to start something on their own."

It sounded like exactly what we needed, so I said, "Get onto it."

Shane spoke to the ex-employees and they entered into discussions with Mintek, the government research agency, to reopen the facility. However, for the ex-employees to make a strong case to Samancor, they were advised that they'd need black partners to meet the BEE requirements. I seemed to be in the right place at the right time, and Shane facilitated a meeting with the ex-employees. While they negotiated the lease of the smelter, I tried to find someone who had a metallurgical background. At the end of 2002, I was introduced to Dr Noel Machingawuta, who worked for Samancor. A Zimbabwean, Noel had a doctorate in metallurgy, and after half an hour of sitting across the desk from him, I knew that he was the man we needed. Noel's measured manner was especially reassuring. After twenty years in England, he still had his Zimbabwean accent, and as we spoke, I remember thinking, "We have to employ this guy on a full-time basis."

Feeling completely at ease with him, I decided to trust my instincts; I told him my life story and shared my dreams of what I envisaged in the BEE arena. Noel agreed to join Leswikeng as a full-time employee. This was a huge commitment from him; even though he had a stable and secure job with Samancor, he was prepared to go out on a limb and join Leswikeng.

That was one of the few times I'd employed someone without going through the appropriate channels, so I had to back-pedal a bit. I called a meeting of the Leswikeng shareholders at the Rosebank Hotel one Saturday in 2002. I explained that the purchase of a 10% share in Mogale Alloys was progressing well, but that it was important for us to have qualified personnel to manage our interests.

"I've met a reputable metallurgist who has agreed to join us in February next year, and I think we're very lucky to have him. But, to retain his services, I think it is only fair to give him an equal shareholding in Leswikeng," I said.

I didn't expect the volcano that erupted in that boardroom.

"I'm not giving away a single percent of my shareholding."

"Why can't we employ him on a contract basis?"

"Why isn't he content with a salary?"

"Give him incentives."

I was stunned.

The Mogale transaction hadn't even been finalised yet, and we were still in the middle of negotiations. I wasn't only astonished at their reaction – I was furious.

"You're being short-sighted," I said. "Instead of thinking about money, you should be thinking about strategy, because at this stage we don't even own a share in Mogale." Leswikeng itself didn't yet own any assets, and already shareholders were greedy. I ignored their pettiness, and because I liked and trusted Noel, I decided to trust my gut feel.

"That's fine, if that's how you feel. It's been nice knowing you all. We can dissolve Leswikeng, We don't have any assets yet, so it will just be a formality," I said and got up to leave. "In fact, keep Leswikeng – I'll form a new company with Noel."

I think that was the moment when the greedy people saw their dreams dissolving in front of their eyes. Some of the more moderate shareholders came over and pleaded with me. Eventually, common sense prevailed. We put it to the vote, and the majority of the shareholders said that they trusted me to do what was best for the company.

The Mogale transaction was negotiated and finalised, and Noel Machingawuta joined Leswikeng as technical director in February 2003. Our business relationship has been very rewarding financially, for both of us. Noel excels at technical issues and is a strategic thinker. I rely on him to explain complicated technical issues, and he accepts that I will make the final business decisions. He is my right-hand man and we trust each other implicitly.

At first, Leswikeng didn't have an office, so Noel and I operated from the Black Like Me premises. Mogale Alloys soon proved to be one of the highlights of Leswikeng, not just because it was the springboard into BEE, but also because of its financial success.

Over time, Noel has become more than a business partner; he is also my friend. We play golf twice a month with Alex Darko – a Ghanaian who moved to Johannesburg when Ashanti concluded a deal with Anglo-American – and my old friend, Louis Mkhetoni. Louis and I have come a long way from the two hungry hustlers we were in Hammanskraal.

Now that I had branched into a new direction with Leswikeng, I needed to make a serious decision regarding my continued involvement in Black Like Me. If I spread myself too thinly, both Leswikeng and Black Like Me would suffer. I was working at the Black Like Me offices, and began to notice things that convinced me management weren't managing the company properly. From the few meetings I attended, and from disgruntled staff members' whispered comments, I realised that there were serious leadership problems. There was not a single leadership figure who inspired the staff, and none of the managers were dynamic enough to steer the company in the direction I wanted. So, rather than allow the company to collapse, I knew I needed to bring in people who were competent – otherwise I'd have to sell Black Like Me again. I mulled over the different configurations and decided I didn't want to sell the company, so I brought in a consultancy firm to analyse Black Like Me and to formulate a strategy to move it forward.

Connie had left the business in 1997 to pursue her education and to take care of our children. When she was awarded her B Com honours degree by Unisa, I felt very proud of her; I was also pleased that she could spend time at home with our two young children while she was studying. But Black Like Me also needed her nurturing, so I asked her to rejoin the company while the consultancy firm was doing its analysis of the business. During this time I had an opportunity to tender for two brands that Unilever were selling – Mentadent P and Close-Up toothpaste.

I had a good working relationship with one of my competitors, Amka Products, and I knew that although they had their own toothpaste brand, they had not been successful in breaking into the toothpaste market.

I called a meeting with Amka, where I outlined the details of the Unilever opportunity. "I suggest we put in a joint bid to buy the brands," I said.

For the next couple of months we worked hard with Amka to put our bid together, and eventually we presented the joint tender. But in the run-up to this, Amka had opened up their factory to me. I was impressed by their extra capacity and systems. Their systems were geared to running various businesses under the same roof, their huge buying power reduced costs, and their streamlined operation was cost-effective. For one thing, I noticed that a pump that cost us over R1 per unit – and we used about 200 000 units a month – Amka imported directly from China at a quarter of the price.

As it turned out, our bid for the toothpaste brands was beaten by Aspen Pharma, who offered substantially more. But all was not lost. The collaboration with Amka had put me in contact with Nizam and Haroon Kalla – excellent potential buyers for Black Like Me. It was early 2005, and by this time Connie had taken over the reins of the company; understandably, she was rather nervous when I approached her and her team with the idea.

"You're asking me to work with another company – but remember what happened with Colgate," Connie said. "I really don't want a repeat performance of that."

"Trust me, Connie," I said to her. "I've seen the operation at Amka, and they know how to run a lean company."

Connie looked at me in silence for a few moments. She was clearly not convinced. "Herman, you of all people will appreciate that I don't want to be dominated by strangers. And I'm only just beginning to enjoy my independence at Black Like Me," she said.

"This is a completely different situation," I said, trying to reassure her. "The big mistake we made with Colgate was allowing the business to stagnate after the take-over. We kept adding staff until our salary bill doubled – and then our production slowed. It won't be like that with Amka, in fact it will be exactly the opposite," I said. "We'll close our manufacturing facility and cut down on staff."

Connie looked at me sceptically. "Are you really saying we must retrench people who have worked for us for a long time? This means they'll lose their jobs, doesn't it?" Connie said, and I had to look away.

Retrenching is never an easy exercise. Some people at Black Like Me had been working there for fifteen years or more; if we sold to Amka, we would have to let go of some of these loyal employees. It was a tough business decision – I knew I had to take advantage of the synergies between Amka and Black Like Me. Our financial director, Nisar Dawood, was also a director and shareholder in Black Like Me, so I called him in and showed him the new business plan; I explained that the new business model no longer required a factory manager, human resource person – or a finance person. It was obvious that a reduction in senior management would translate into massive savings to the company. But, still, it was not easy to say to Nisar, "It's a hard decision, but this is the route I am forced to take." At the end of the 49% sell-out to Amka, only ten out of the ninety personnel from Black Like Me kept their jobs.

I decided that the best way to retrench staff was through consultation. This would enable us to talk people through the process and to deal with the situation honestly. I was completely upfront with the staff, and I explained the issues that Black Like Me needed to deal with, as well as the advantages to the company of retrenchment. I stood in front of loyal members of staff and told them, "I've always managed to keep Black Like Me afloat – and there have been some very rough patches. But we've lost market share, and I don't have the money to rescue the company. There's another problem too: I have moved into other business commitments. This time, if Black Like Me collapses, all of you are going to lose out. The best thing to do is to sell out a share to Amka so as to get the business up to par again." This was not an easy moment, so the best thing was to put the facts on the table clearly and dispassionately.

Soon afterwards, Amka held interviews for staff who wished to be employed at the Amka facility. Those who weren't absorbed into the new company were paid retrenchment packages.

Connie's anxiety about the union was short-lived, and she continues to thrive in her role as Managing Director of Black Like Me. The Amka/Black Like Me operation is well co-ordinated, and Connie has successfully divided her time between work and home, giving both the time they need and deserve.

Chapter 17

Black Like Me was behind me, and I now looked ahead to building up a BEE investment portfolio. But, looking back a few years, after Leswikeng's successful buy-in into Mogale in 2002, I realise that I'd got a taste of something new and exciting – the negotiations and the new environment stimulated and interested me. With Noel Machingawuta as Leswikeng's technical director, and Charmaine Rayson as my secretary, I moved into a small office where Leswikeng could be run independently.

Getting into the BEE investment arena in 2002 was helped along by a network of corporate people I had known for ten years. Many of these connections were established in 1992, when I'd been invited to join the Johannesburg Chapter of the Young Presidents Organisation (YPO), which comprised about 200 young business presidents. The YPO is an international organisation dedicated to providing a nurturing environment for young CEOs. At the time I was invited to join, there were no other black members. I was one of ten people who comprised a forum, which met once a month. Rod Fehrsen from the PG group, Myra Salkinder from Kirsh Industries, Sam Hackner from Investec, and Idris Hathurani, the founder of Jumbo Cash & Carry, were among the members in my group. During our four-hour forum meetings we got to know each other well, sharing family issues and business frustrations without fear of judgement, and all in the strictest confidence. We also supported and advised one another regarding our various business difficulties – and the advice often differed from that given by fellow board members of our respective companies. In the forum there was no competition, no self-interest – the good, solid advice came from people who had a different perspective and whose distance from a problem lent objectivity. I found this sounding board very refreshing and helpful; as a result of our intimate interaction, we all became close friends.

A business network is crucial to any entrepreneur's success, as I had understood from my earliest days of selling linen and crockery from the boot of my car. My experience at the YPO confirmed this, as it provided wider opportunities when I started Leswikeng. I told everyone I knew what I was doing, and in this way I hoped that the right opportunity would arrive. My instinct proved to be correct. Soon afterwards, my friend Kholekile Biyana – who had built my house in Soshanguve, my factory in Mabopane, and made extensions to my Midrand factory – arranged a meeting with the CEO of Stocks Building Africa. The CEO, Tom Henry, had read stories about my emergence into the BEE arena, and he had asked my friend to introduce us.

At first, I was doubtful about the advantage of such a meeting. "But Stocks are in construction," I said. "As you know, I've just sold out a percentage of my haircare business, and I've invested in the ferrochrome industry – and, in any case, what do I know about the building industry?" But my curiosity had been aroused, and I agreed to meet the Stocks CEO.

Tom Henry was an Irishman who had lived in South Africa for over thirty years. He still had a broad Irish accent, and I struggled at times to understand what he was saying. But I found his warmth appealing – and we both loved British soccer. So, although I had reservations about what I could offer a construction company, I liked Tom, and I was interested to see where our discussions would take us.

"Forget about your lack of knowledge of the industry," Tom said. "The important thing is that you know how to make money.

You're a dealmaker – never forget that."

It felt good to meet a man who was so encouraging and who saw my strengths – and pointed out how these strengths might add value to his business. I always say that I haven't really had a mentor in my life, but insofar as a mentor guides and teaches, I would have to say that Tom Henry came the closest to playing this role. He was a natural mentor, it was part of his personality, and I suspect that he has been a positive influence in the lives of many other people who met him.

It didn't take long for Tom to persuade me to become a shareholder in Stocks Building Africa and soon afterwards Shane Ferguson structured an attractive deal. Tom then introduced me to RMB Ventures, who were the major shareholders. RMB owned 72% of Stocks, and because I wanted to buy 30% of the company, I needed to buy some shares from RMB Ventures. Shane Ferguson joined me at the preliminary meeting with RMB Ventures – which didn't last even ten minutes. Whenever Shane and I talk about that first meeting, he always says, "The meeting was finished before we'd finished our coffee!" Of course, the meeting was so brief because our opening bid was so far below RMB's expectations. Later that day, Tom called me at my office and invited me over, and for the next few months he and I worked hard to close the gap between what Leswikeng was prepared to offer and RMB's price tag on the 30% I was after. A few months later we struck a deal, and I was invited to attend the next Stocks board meeting.

I was excited about it all, but at the same time I felt out of my depth. I admitted as much to Connie one evening, "How will I manage with all those highly educated board members? Most of them don't have just one degree, they have two or three."

Connie smiled and said, "You are streetwise and wise, Herman. That's got you where you are today. People like you don't need certificates to prove their competence."

As part of the deal I was elected chairman of the board. Though

Connie had reassured me that my kind of experience couldn't be bought at any university, I still had the feeling of being in unfamiliar territory. I asked Tom to chair the first meeting so that I could familiarise myself with the company's protocol; he graciously agreed, and so began a friendship that lasted until Tom died of cancer some years later.

Tom had told me that I knew how to make money; I often thought about this, and it guided me in making decisions about Leswikeng's acquisitions. Though I am aware of my responsibility to my fellow partners, I instinctively seek out new investments that adhere to the basic business tenet of making a profit. I am not prepared to collaborate with cowboys who come to me and say, "Mr Mashaba, if you fund my business I will create many new jobs." It makes me angry when people looking for finance say what they think I want to hear instead of providing a viable business plan.

I have so often been in situations where I have had to say, "Who do you think you are fooling? You've given me every reason why I should finance you – so that your new business can create jobs, or that I really need to fund your product or service because there is a market for them – but you haven't given me the only reason I want to hear." I have always ended these discussions with the words, "The bottom line is, if you are not in business to make money, then I do not want to be your partner."

Wealth creation has to be the single motivating factor for any executive. It is only when your business is profitable that you can employ people.

I have never employed people simply because I want to give them a job. If this were the case, I would have employed my brother Pobane – or any number of extended family members who battle even today to secure employment. I do not look after my senior staff members simply because I like them – I look after them because I believe that they are expertly equipped to develop and protect my assets.

Many critics have accused me of being inconsistent in my choice of investments. According to these critics, the portfolios are too diverse; also, my investments are unmanageable, and I focus on private companies rather than corporates. Yet, my choices have been deliberate and strategic. When I started Black Like Me, I chose partners who put a good package on the table and were people I clicked with; if there is no chemistry between people, the business relationship is doomed. Usually, I meet with the CEO – as I did with Tom Henry – and if there's a rapport between us, and I have a good feeling about the company's performance, we proceed to negotiations. From there, the dialogue progresses fairly smoothly and without too much delay because we don't have the red tape of the corporate machine that goes with the listed companies. I also don't want to be stifled by having the same set of partners, which is why I set up the Phatsima Group and Lephatsi Investments; by expanding my partnership groupings I am able to diversify the different company investments.

Another important element is the liquidity of a company. Where at all possible, my partners and I try to incur the lowest debt when investing in a new company. I look at companies that have a strong turnover; this ensures that the investment debt can be serviced and quickly liquidated so that investors can start earning dividends early on. These are all important aspects of my business investment model.

Leswikeng, Phatsima and Lephatsi – my three Broad-Based Black Economic Empowerment (BBBEE) initiatives – have shareholdings in a diverse portfolio of companies spanning mining, construction, aeronautics, finance and information technology. The vision of each is to become a leading non-racial entrepreneurial and socially responsible company, and to be at the forefront of the economic empowerment of previously disadvantaged groups in South Africa. To this end, their mission is to make a positive contribution to all the businesses we invest in.

BEE and BBBEE are different yet essential tools for transforming the South African economy. BEE measures equity ownership and management representation, but BBBEE seeks to distribute wealth across a broad spectrum of South African society. I am convinced that both will improve the lives of ordinary South Africans. But BBBEE can succeed only if there are properly trained employees.

The South African manufacturing sector has severely declined over recent decades, and South Africa needs a second industrial revolution to boost development and make it sustainable. To achieve this, South Africans need to integrate new technologies and machinery into educational institutions so that we can prepare our learners for life in the real world. If we fail to produce much-needed technical experts, we will have a nation of polarised youngsters: on the one hand, a group of achievers who seek only to enter the corporate or professional world, and, on the other hand, a group of under-achievers who cannot provide for themselves because they don't have the skills. Unskilled workers – and my brother Pobane was one of them – are not equipped for life in the commercial sector. These workers are generally under-achievers because neither educational institutions nor corporate and private companies are equipping them with the kinds of skills they need to take their rightful place in the economy.

There are various ways in which the broad vision of black empowerment – the creation of black business and management opportunities – may be realised. These include legislation, but also help from government and business. But it will also require boldness on the part of black professionals to seize these opportunities and make the most of them. Certainly, there is a need in our economy for more risks to be taken, and for the self-complacency that comes with secure positions to be replaced with creative initiatives that could change the contours of the business landscape in South Africa.

The government has made significant strides in encouraging and increasing black operational participation and control in the economy, specifically in the realm of government tenders. But unfortunately there are always lazy and dishonest people who seek ways of making money with no effort. Some have taken advantage of the tender system by acting as black fronts for white companies, thereby doing black business a great disservice, as this effectively keeps operational control in white hands. This merely frustrates the participation of black people in the economy and slows the expansion of production.

BBBEE is a government initiative which recognises that our democracy cannot survive as long as the majority of black people remain on the periphery of wealth-sharing. The challenge for business is to act swiftly by embracing BBBEE; any delay will encourage political instability, which will inevitably reverse the gains of the liberation struggle. Liberation is what our grandfathers and grandmothers, our fathers and mothers, our aunts and uncles, sisters and brothers fought for, and it is a fight we must continue. We have won democratic freedom, now we must win economic freedom.

Chapter 18

"What is the one thing that is common to all entrepreneurs?" I have been asked this question a million times, by everyone from schoolchildren and housewives to senior executives, and it is a question that always makes me smile. They want me to supply that elusive magic ingredient that they hope will provide them with a 100% guarantee for a successful business. But the reality is: there is no one single ingredient.

Every successful entrepreneur has his or her own unique story. Education is an important factor. My own education was basic, but Mark Shuttleworth, who established Thawte and made enough money from the sale of his business to become an astronaut, was privileged to attend excellent schools and to complete his university career. In my case, I saw a gap in the black haircare market; Robert Brozin, the founder of Nando's, had a love of good food. Each entrepreneur has different likes and dislikes, different management styles, and diverse skills; and ultimately, we all have our own ideal of success. While I don't believe that one aspect of entrepreneurship should be elevated above another, I do believe that each has its own role to play during the various stages of a business career.

Versatility is an important facet of entrepreneurship, and when I started Black Like Me, this quality was the key to stabilising the company – I had to fit in wherever I was needed. And, of course, salesmanship is my forte, and along the way, I learnt and perfected the skills of marketing and customer satisfaction. My early foray into the BEE space demanded that I up my corporate game as I didn't have the educational pedigree of my colleagues. This was a sore point, and often after a long day in the boardroom, I'd come home and unburden myself. "What am I doing with these people?" I'd say to Connie. "I am not qualified for this." In her usual way, Connie was supportive and reassuring as I waded into new waters.

Mentors are invaluable to personal development, and I was fortunate to have had good mentors like Walter Dube and Tom Henry, both of whom helped me to fill in gaps in my knowledge. I have always tried to learn from successful people, and whenever anyone asks me for tips on improving their business skills, I say, "Read. Read. Read." Earlier on, I mentioned how important Raymond Ackerman's autobiography was to me. By reading about his personal journey, I learnt that hardship can be a blessing in disguise – as it was when Ackerman was fired from Shoprite. Undaunted, he went on to found Pick n Pay, thereby revolutionising the consumer experience in South Africa. Ackerman's story showed me the importance of believing in oneself and working hard to achieve one's goals.

Richard Branson is another exceptional businessman who, like me, had no tertiary educational qualifications to speak of. His autobiography, *Losing My Virginity*, describes growing up in a society where the lack of education should have been a hindrance to success, and his refusal to allow these shortcomings to define him. Branson held firmly to his ideas, he worked hard to implement them, and the Virgin brand developed into one of the world's most extraordinary success stories.

Another inspiring story of success is Felicia Mabuza-Suttle's autobiography, *Dare to Dream*. In it, she tells the story of a girl who grew up in the dusty streets of Soweto and pursued her dream; she was determined to get a higher education, to prove apartheid's ideologies wrong. She achieved her goal, earning herself a BA, an MA and a PhD, and the last I heard, this remarkable woman was reading for a second doctorate – this time in business administration.

One day my nephew, who had dropped out of his engineering course, came to see me. "Please, malome, can you please fund me – I want to change courses."

I gave him a chance to explain. "First, you will have to tell me why you did this," I said. "Also, what is it that you want to study?"

"Engineering is boring. I want to go and study entrepreneurship at a college," he said.

"Listen, it's not enough just to want to become an entrepreneur," I said somewhat angrily. He was clearly surprised at my reaction, and I went on, "Do you think that entrepreneurship is something that you can just go to a university and learn? No, man, you've got to have the aptitude. It's not like engineering, or law – it demands creative flair, vision. Have you got that?"

I went on to explain the importance of luck, and of being able to think on your feet, which are not things that can be taught – you either get a break or you don't, and you either have the ability to react sharply or you don't. I told him that almost every opportunity that has come my way has been something I have reacted to immediately – if you hesitate, you lose out.

There are excellent tertiary business, marketing and sales courses, but none of them can teach gut instinct or belief in oneself – these are intangibles that a person either possesses or they don't. I don't believe that there is a college in the world that can teach business instinct. But there are certain basics that any potential enterpreneur needs, and this is why I give financial support to the St Mary's Alexandra School Project. This project buses about eighty Grade 10 learners from five different schools in Alex to St Mary's School in Waverley, where they are taught Maths, Physical Science, Life Sciences, Geography and English, as well as being provided with textbooks and stationery. The

2009 class proved the success of this kind of venture when it achieved an 88% pass rate.

Apart from such basic education initiatives, I also support initiatives where aspirant enterpreneurs can discuss the meaning of entrepreneurship, where people like me can tell our own stories and those of other successful entrepreneurs. There are many inspiring stories, including those of Sol Kerzner, who introduced affordable resort holidays to South Africans and soon became an international hotel tycoon, and Donald Gordon, a visionary and philanthropist who changed the face of the South African insurance industry. These are men who believed in themselves and their vision. But entrepreneurs are not islands, they cannot succeed without help along the way.

Two people who helped me enormously during the early days of my career were Steve and Heather Gustafson. With their help, I was able to upgrade my sales techniques. The entrepreneur continually needs to develop new skills in order to cope with the changing business landscape. Nothing happens in a vacuum and without outside help of some sort. There needs to be a more positive climate, with access to business infrastructure such as offices and warehouses, and also to manufacturers, as well as to training programmes; such access will assist entrepreneurs enormously in developing their skills.

One important area where entrepreneurs need assistance is finance. In the 1980s there was an advert for a financial institution depicting a white bank manager greeting his white customers – an image that has stuck in my mind. With the emergent black middle class, people have more disposable income than before; the banks are happy to take their money, but there is still a reluctance to provide adequate business loans for black customers. This is, I believe, a result of the continued dominance of white males, in particular, in decision-making roles at our financial institutions. In addition to this, there is a general lack of confidence in black people, and bank officials seem to doubt that blacks have the necessary collateral to back up their loan applications. The access of black people to loans will continue to be limited under current circumstances, unless concrete changes are implemented to assist blacks in building wealth. It frustrates me to see that many dreams will never be realised, and for no other reason than blacks are perceived as being bad credit risks. This attitude is creating a generation of economically disadvantaged people.

I am an unashamed capitalist, and I wish that South Africans would appreciate the good fortune they have to be living in a democratic, capitalist society which is a fertile environment for entrepreneurs. If South Africa's tradition of entrepreneurship is embraced by those with the capital needed to build the economy, we will start to see huge strides in the growth of the country. The government needs to nurture black entrepreneurs – but this doesn't simply entail the establishment of colleges that include business theory and entrepreneurship in their curricula. When I am approached by family members or friends to support their children's education, I am willing and eager to do so, but I always insist that the young people follow credible courses.

My current secretary, Charmaine Rayson, has the unenviable task of screening my calls; she is inundated with requests from people wanting me to support them in their studies or in their new businesses. She recently forwarded me an email from a young Zimbabwean student who had been accepted to study actuarial science at the University of Pretoria, but did not have the financial wherewithal to pay her fees. Charmaine arranged a meeting with the young woman, and I agreed to help her. My decision to pay not only the fees, but also to provide her with a subsistence allowance, was based on many factors: the young woman had been pro-active in finding someone to assist her with the fees her family could not afford, and she had refused to yield to the restraints of poverty. Africa needs the intellectual capital of young people like this who are both smart and determined.

It saddens me whenever I visit the isolated rural areas of South Africa and I encounter young men and women who cannot find work because they live far from job opportunities, in remote areas that are out of sight and out of mind of both government and business. In South Africa today, revitalising the rural economy remains one of our biggest challenges. The government's rural development strategy that is underway at present is simply not enough. Its focus is on infrastructure development, support for emergent black farmers and the subsistence economy, rebuilding social services infrastructure such as schools and clinics, and the provision of clean water. Of course, these things make an important contribution by creating appropriate conditions for economic empowerment and job creation. But entrepreneurs can add value to these development programmes by identifying opportunities, and realising them. If entrepreneurs are given the chance of finding effective means and methods of contributing to rural development, they will play a vital role in halting further stagnation and eliminating poverty. They will be able to create productive bases for industrialisation and the modernisation of rural economies in South Africa.

Crime remains an area of concern, however, and business is often frustrated and even destroyed by the high incidence of crime – both white-collar and blue-collar. Stock losses can cripple businesses and put them under such financial stress that they are unable to recover. During my time with Black Like Me, robberies in the townships forced me to discontinue the credit system to many township customers whose businesses were robbed, making it impossible for them to pay me for stock. If business in general, and black business in particular, is to succeed, we have to work towards creating stability in our communities. Sustainable enterprises can only flourish under conditions of peace in our daily lives. The political stability and maturity that we are rightfully so proud of must be coupled with social stability and concerted efforts on the part of the entire criminal justice system to rid our communities of crime. Our success can be permanent only if we are all full participants in efforts to change our lives for the better. To this end, we need to form strong networks to protect entrepreneurship, and to ensure that it thrives.

I am fortunate to do business with many international companies, from whom I have learnt much. I appreciate the Kaizen business philosophy of the Japanese, which focuses on making continuous small improvements that keep a business at the top of its game, and I also respect the German post-war commitment to modernisation – which I believe needs to happen in post-apartheid South Africa. However, I believe that South Africans should maintain their own identity. South Africa has absolutely no need to imitate any other nation's model. South Africa is its own special brand, and labour, business and civil society have all been active participants in inventing our unique South African imprint – which was especially obvious during the 2010 Soccer World Cup.

To reiterate, South Africa embraces the capitalist system, and the role of business is to create wealth, which can in turn benefit the general community through job creation and the development of the economy. Hosting the 2010 Soccer World Cup saw an upgrade of infrastructure nationally, and their construction created employment for many skilled people. We also benefited from the importation of foreign skills, especially in the upgrading of roads, and the local workforce benefited from exposure to these imported engineering skills. The World Cup also introduced our many tourism destinations and our friendly citizens to the world. The vuvuzela may have been the signature of our supporters, but our professionalism, affability and ability to deliver showed the world what South Africa is capable of.

The government has created conditions conducive to growth. But it is up to all economically active South Africans to work hard to prevent the economy stagnating. The government also tried to create a reasonably flexible labour market dispensation, which would encourage the labour movement to be well organised and strong enough to improve the conditions of workers; this initially compared favourably with those of other developing countries, but I am convinced that we need to revisit our current labour laws if we are to ensure that they achieve the results that were originally intended. In such an environment, businesses would have the necessary freedom to make profits and to prosper. Of course, the challenge is to strike a healthy balance between the interests of the business sector and those of a society in transformation. Without such a balance, we run the risk of unending economic skirmishes, which might cumulatively defeat the overall objective of growing and developing a sound economy.

The government has enacted the economic policies necessary to realising the success of our country, but civil society has an important role to play in mobilising communities. Business leaders must empower their workers to realise their full potential. In turn, these employees must empower their families, by encouraging attendance at schools and participation in educational and social activities. Everyone should strive for excellence in what they do, and encourage and teach others who lack skills. This will ensure meaningful and inclusive participation. Communities that support each other will sustain the growth of our entrepreneurship and our economy.

One way I try to help young entrepreneurs is by talking to them – at schools, in universities and in the workplace. I don't have all the answers, but I do have my own experiences, and some of these may resonate with people experiencing similar problems. One group I am especially proud to be involved with is employees from the PG group; I mentor and share knowledge in an informal way with PG employees who are interested in empowering themselves. It often concerns me when people say that, because they're employed in a bread-and-butter job, they can't be entrepreneurs. But this is simply not true. Everyone has a dream – perhaps even the lady who makes tea at your office. Who knows? She may dream of opening a daycare centre. But my job is not to hold her hand through every step she would need to take. As a mentor, my job is to teach such a person the value of having a vision, and to show what steps are needed to get the appropriate qualification or experience that will propel them in the direction of realising that vision. When people share similar hopes and dreams, they can often work with and for one another to help realise their individual visions.

I enjoy working with journalists and writers who publish stories about entrepreneurs, and I frequently take part in radio shows about current affairs or business programmes. And though I have come to enjoy the game of golf enormously, I will even give up a game to do such shows. Now and again I have to put up with the resentment of friends and colleagues, who say, "Oh no, you don't need to do another TV talk show, everyone knows who you are." I smile at this, but don't explain that these efforts have nothing to do with building my personal platform. By now, I have established myself. I do the interviews, the talks, the one-on-one mentoring, the books and the articles because I see them as an opportunity to reach a wider audience, to reach readers and listeners who wish to hone their skills, their talents, their education – whatever it is they need to help them realise the vision they have for themselves.

I give talks to a range of people, from township schoolchildren to international business forums – including business schools in South Africa, the St Gallen Business School in Switzerland, and Oxford University. Across the world, in all places, people strive for success; I feel privileged to be in a position where I can share my knowledge and experience to help others achieve their goals.

Chapter 19

At Black Like Me, we took our corporate responsibility seriously – offering bursaries to needy students and sponsoring political funerals. In terms of career building, we used to pack up product samples and literature and hit the road, going into communities and training hairdressers, improving their product knowledge and their skills. We were already very busy with various forms of community upliftment, so I was hesitant when Rod Fehrsen approached me yet again in 1997 to become a patron of the Field Band Foundation (FBF) – a worthy organisation aimed at uplifting black children and, by extension, their families.

The previous year, the PG Group had celebrated its centenary. It had decided to establish a community upliftment project – but it wanted to ensure that it would also be meaningful and sustainable. Rod had approached me about this, saying, "I want to have the best people involved in the project. We need some creative thinkers to brainstorm ideas and to throw around a couple of innovative concepts. This is an important project for two guys, Bertie and Ronnie Lubner. I really hope you'll join us."

PG had contracted a consultant, who came up with the idea of the Field Band Foundation, and R6 million was allocated to the project. At the time, after the Colgate buy-out, I had my hands fairly full with Black Like Me and its own corporate responsibility programmes. So I tried to put Rod off by saying, "I don't know if I can manage it; my time is so limited."

The affable Rod would not be deterred, however. "I tell you what, Herman, you just come along and see what we're doing."

Some people refuse to take no for an answer, and Rod is one of them. I ended up agreeing to come on board. Ever since our involvement in the YPO, Rod and I had shared similar views about social and business reform, so I was optimistic that I'd be involved in a project that would be driven by men and women who were committed and enthusiastic.

I'd tried hard to convince Rod that I was not the right person for the job. I'd told him that even though I loved all kinds of music, I wasn't musically talented. But Rod was far too persuasive, and in the end I was made patron of the FBF. I was invited to attend the first board meeting, and while we sat around the table discussing the project, I felt my excitement growing and I fell in love with what they envisaged. Ever since, I have ensured that I am available to attend the quarterly board meetings. The FBF relies on voluntary commitment, and I have learnt from experience that when people are not paid for their participation, organisations do not always enjoy the commitment they deserve. I was determined not to fail in my commitment.

I took my entire family to watch the first Field Band National Championships. It was a really thrilling event held at Wits University, and when we arrived at the stadium the car park was already filled with mini-buses, cars and buses that had transported the bands to the jamboree; participants were fussing with last-minute touches to colourful costumes, and carrying instruments that were sometimes bigger than the children who played them. The stadium buzzed with excitement. The memories of my own childhood rushed back, and I was mesmerised.

In the open-air stadium, we took our seats amidst excited, clapping families and friends; it was wonderful to be out in the fresh air with Connie and the children, away from corporate demands and air-conditioned offices. The jamboree began with bands marching around the stadium. What a sight it was! Hundreds of boys and girls paraded past us, decked out in uniforms that we could only have dreamt of as children; in their smiles and cocky manner, I remembered a younger Herman – my heart beating as wildly as my drum. I watched as a variety of band members marched past us, tall and small, black and white, flamboyantly dressed or simply clothed. All of them were beaming with delight, and the spectators whistled and ululated in appreciation.

Proud and happy, we joined in the wild applause for the talented and committed children who had come from all over the country, most of them from homes no better than the humble one I'd grown up in. Their performances were especially remarkable considering the severely disadvantaged backgrounds they came from, where many parents were unemployed, and where there was barely money for food, let alone the very expensive musical instruments. Yet there the kids were on the field that day, blowing their shiny tubas and beating kettledrums, making music as if they had been taught at a music conservatory or any one of the private schools in the elite suburbs; they danced as if their bones were elastic.

Those children had poured their hearts and souls into their performances, reminding me that South Africans really do know how to celebrate life with dance and song – reminding me of *Ipi Ntombi* all those years ago. The thrills of the day had completely exceeded my expectations, and we all decided that we would definitely be at the next event, whether or not we were invited. If this spectacle was what social responsibility and upliftment programmes were about, then I was proud to be a part of it. At the end of the day I returned home with a smile and a melody in my heart instead of a corporate frown. And long after the performance, I could still hear the percussion instruments in my ears, and see the sequined costumes flashing in the sunlight. It had also been a real pleasure to be involved in something that my family could enjoy with me. But, most importantly, from a business point of view, I had seen with my own eyes that well-developed and carefully managed social development programmes are more than just struggling charities – they are strong instruments for personal development, social integration, and the future growth of communities.

Today, the FBF has more than four thousand children participating in programmes that are run in all nine provinces. There are no criteria for participation other than commitment; it does not matter if a participant does not have shoes or has never played a musical instrument, and it does not even matter if they cannot walk – there are active members of the FBF who are physically disabled. If a child wants to participate, the leaders will find a home for their talent, whether it is acrobatics or tapping away at a triangle – everybody has to start somewhere. Many of the leaders of the programme are former FBF members who have risen up through the Foundation and been sent on leadership workshops and training programmes that enable them to teach other children.

For the past four years I have been chairperson of the FBF, and I am happy to carry out the commitment I have made to the Foundation. The FBF does not run on goodwill alone, it runs on strict business principles and is extremely fortunate to have committed sponsors. Anyone who buys a lottery ticket automatically supports the FBF, as it is a beneficiary of the National Lottery Distribution Trust Fund. Several other companies and organisations fund the FBF, including De Beers and PG – but it's important to say that people also devote time to the Foundation. Funds are always carefully managed, as accountability is a major consideration when I decide to get involved in a project; I want to see where the money is going, and I am not interested in participating if only 10c out of every R1 that is donated goes to the programme. If the project cannot show me that it is capable of judicious management, I am not interested in getting involved. It is simply not good enough for sponsored money to be funnelled into the project manager's private bank account; this money has been given in good faith. Managers earn a salary, and if it is a good salary, nobody will mind – but only if the managers do their job properly.

The FBF has been farsighted in recognising that its child members are part of a greater community, and it currently leases a property in Eshowe to house the FBF academy. The Foundation has always dreamed big dreams for its members, and many talented FBF members travel to Norway, Belgium and the United States every year to participate in international events. The Norges Musikkorps Forbund (Norway), Vlamo (Belgium), and Pioneer Drum Corps (USA) have been excellent partners in helping the FBF to achieve high standards. All of these overseas organisations have sent experienced trainers to South Africa to train local leaders and band instructors, helping to upgrade their skills. It is gratifying to attend these workshops and to see how the interaction benefits our members, with the useful spin-off of helping to develop committed and empowered local leaders.

When our members travel overseas to perform, they impress audiences, not only with their talent, but also with their unique enthusiasm. The FBF impressed a broad range of international audiences when it participated in the 2010 World Cup celebrations during the countdown festivities. A total of 371 FBF members also performed in the opening and closing ceremonies. This memorable experience boosted the confidence of all its members, not only those who actually performed, but also those who aspire to perform in similar international events.

The person behind the FBF is Bertie Lubner, a man I would have chosen to be my father, if such a thing were possible. Shortly after my conversation with Rod Fehrsen, Bertie and his wife, Hilary, invited Connie and me to their home for breakfast, and it was wonderful to be surrounded by their close-knit family. Soon afterwards, Bertie asked me to sit on the board of the FBF, and there was no way I could refuse a man who is dedicated to making a difference in the lives of black children. Over the years, we have met up with one another at the Field Band events, where I have seen Bertie weep tears of joy as he watches the kids; a stranger would hardly believe that he is a son of the one of the wealthiest families in South Africa. Bertie Lubner gives his whole heart to projects that are creating change in South Africa. But apart from Bertie's big heart, I have also come to admire his enormous business acumen, which I have witnessed while attending PG board meetings. Whenever I feel glum about the mouthing off of an irrational politician, to this day, a single positive comment from Bertie reassures me.

Black Like Me has spawned an initiative called Black Like Us (BLU). It is an art initiative that works with professional artists, helping to improve their business skills so that they can earn a living from their art. BLU arose out of a phone call that I received in 2003 from Maureen Dixon of the Watercolour Society of South Africa, asking me to assist them with their arts programme. My initial impression was that I would be expected to support struggling artists, but when I met the Watercolour Society's management team, I was really impressed with the vision they sketched of our involvement. The Watercolour Society is regularly approached by artists in need of assistance, whether by way of sponsorship of materials or exposure of their work; eventually, the Watercolour Society of South Africa came up with a plan for formalising its participation in this empowerment of black artists.

Creative people are unique; they are so absorbed with the creative process that they do not always know how to attend to the business side of their profession. But I decided that if Black Like Me was going to be involved in the initiative, I wanted to be sure that the artists themselves recognised the need to learn how to manage the business side of their activities.

At the first meeting I attended, I addressed the artists present and explained that we wanted to help them fulfil their potential; shortly after my address, Abe Mathabe stood up and said that, as an artist, he could also help by teaching skills and techniques to new artists. But before he finished, I stood up and said, "Stop right there! I am not a communist; I am a capitalist, and the only way of raising the status of artists is to teach them how to make money out of their art."

I am unapologetic in my approach: it is pointless to produce beautiful art if you cannot afford to feed your family off the proceeds. My key philosophy is that if you do not look after yourself, then you cannot look after anyone else. Also, I am a hardworking executive; and it is precisely my life-long work ethic that has freed me up to participate in and sponsor programmes such as the FBF and BLU art initiative.

Black Like Us took my advice and, ever since, each artist who participates in the programme is provided with expert advice and a starter pack of artist's materials. Depending on their individual needs, they are also provided with advice as to how they can market themselves, and each artist is also supplied with an order book. So, when the artists deliver their artworks to a gallery, they are able to provide the gallery owner with an invoice of the art they have given on consignment. It is this kind of practical business tool that has helped to build up a team of professional artists who are properly paid for their hard work and exceptional talent. People with expert business skills are well paid, and there is no reason why excellent artists should not be equally well paid for their cultural contribution.

Black Like Us has supported many artists in improving their careers, and today some of them have even achieved international recognition. Abe Mathabe is a typical Black Like Us artist. He grew up in Pimville, in a large family whose focus was on survival, putting food on the table, and caught up as they were in this, there was not much time left to devote to social interaction among family members – or, indeed, to recognise Abe's budding talent. Abe had trained as a signwriter and one day, feeling frustrated and wishing to express himself on paper, he rummaged around the house until he found a Bic ballpoint pen; he used the pen to make a beautiful, delicate line drawing, and since then he has never looked back. His background in graphic art helped him to make the crisp drawings that charmed the artists at the Watercolour Society of South Africa. They immediately agreed to represent his work. A curator of the society's arts programme, Zanne Bezuidenhoudt, saw something unique in Abe's drawings, recognising that the delicate scale of the work lent itself to miniaturist art. She encouraged Abe to consider trying his hand at this demanding art form, and Abe's miniatures are now internationally acclaimed. He was recently an honoured guest at the annual miniaturist exhibition in Tasmania, Australia.

I have never had an art lesson, and I certainly do not have the expertise to recognise the potential in these talented men and women of the BLU art programme. What I do have, however, is the means to sponsor their unique talents, thus enabling them to develop their careers.

There are many people who have been helped through programmes such as BLU. But assisting individuals and sponsoring cultural programmes should not be seen in isolation; these are integral to the broader evolution of society – which is itself the result of such cultural programmes. South Africa cannot rely for its development on political reform alone; all countries need social reform, and to progress as evolved citizens, we need to participate in activities that encourage the development of the arts and also sports. This will have far-reaching benefits for the psyche of our nation. One has only to remember the 1995 Rugby World Cup, and how at the time it united many citizens who reached over the rift caused by apartheid. More recently, South Africans joined hands to welcome foreign tourists during the 2010 World Cup.

It is not humanly possible to be involved in every programme that is brought to my attention. I simply do not have the time and, to be quite honest, some programmes do not appeal to me. In some cases I give a donation to solve a particular problem, and at other times I am called upon to offer mentorship. One thing that means a lot to me is mentorship; I take every opportunity to do so, as I suspect that many of my childhood and university friends may have achieved more if they had enjoyed the support of a mentor – though, of course, GaRamotse was a completely different time, a different place.

I recently received a request from the headmaster of Ratshepo High School, my old school in Temba. He asked me to pay a visit to see if there was any way I could assist with the upgrading of the school. I drove to Temba, rather reluctantly, I must admit. Going back to visit family and good friends is a pleasure, but driving through familiar streets and seeing the same forlorn faces that I'd left behind thirty years ago can be quite soul-destroying. I find myself wondering what blessed star I was born under, why was I singled out to live a successful life, and yet friends like Shakes, my old soccer pal, are still wandering aimlessly around the village. But then I remind myself of what I had to sacrifice and how stubborn I needed to be to succeed; even so, this does not ease the sorrow I feel each time I return to Hammanskraal.

I did not know what to expect at Ratshepo High, which had certainly never been a prosperous school. When I arrived, I was met by the headmaster, Peter Maswanganye, and the local education inspector. They took me on a tour of the school. I was concerned with the over-crowding in the classes, as some classrooms housed ninety-two pupils. My worry was that if I built the three extra classrooms the headmaster felt they needed, who would provide the additional requirements? If I sponsored new buildings at the school, that would only be the beginning; where would the rest of the requirements come from – the equipment, the books, the sports facilities? At the time of my visit in 2008, I was chairman of Stocks, and so I was in a position to try to persuade businesses to sponsor a revitalisation project at the school. But on the drive home, as I mulled over the headmaster's appeal, I realised that, quite honestly, the project was too big for me. The government has neglected many rural schools, it is no longer putting enough energy and resources into them because urban schools are far more demanding and have higher enrolment numbers. Just because Ratshepo was my old high school did not mean that I should abandon my beliefs in good business practice.

I refused to allow sentiment to sway my instincts, so I turned down the request for help. It was a moment of personal regret, but a decision had to be made on feasibility; even though I may have been able to pull it off, the project did not have the elements necessary to ensure its sustainability. Both FBF and BLU are accountable and sustainable initiatives; the money put into them is converted into projects and measurable results which ultimately outperform the sponsorship amounts. Regrettably, my old high school did not seem to have the potential to perform in the same way.

Involvement in any social programme requires sacrifices, and it is an unfortunate fact that in most instances the sacrifices have been made by my family. While I am out mentoring or lecturing or visiting social programmes, I have to leave my family to carry on with their own lives. For some programmes demand more than money, they demand my presence and personal hands-on activity.

In 2007, the PG group asked me to initiate a short programme for a group of their employees, which I agreed to do. The programme was well received and the participants wanted me to continue for a while, which I again agreed to – thinking that it would only last a few more months at most. Four years later, I am still meeting the group one evening every month. It's not a SETA-approved programme, and it is certainly not designed for PG employees to increase their output so that the company makes more glass; it is much more than that. Sometimes I bring along a guest speaker, or I talk about the power of reading, and we discuss books that we have read; at other times we have discussions on a variety of topics, for example, how to resolve social or corporate issues.

While many companies have corporate indabas, most employees do not really have the opportunity of bringing other aspects of their lives into the workplace; they generally see themselves as part of the company rather than as individuals. It is all very well to expect employees to perform at peak productivity, but employees are individual human beings who want to play Action Cricket, or buy a new home, or start a literacy programme; they dream of owning a café, or of climbing Mount Kilimanjaro. These individual needs and wants must be recognised and encouraged, so that employees have properly developed psyches. It is highly unlikely that the assembly-line worker who screws on bottle tops actually likes screwing on bottle tops, so what does he like, what are his dreams, and how can we help him to realise those dreams while he's an employee? That is the kind of thing that real empowerment is all about.

The PG employee programme is an excellent forum for engagement, and I have seen its men and women commit themselves to setting and reaching personal goals. Their ideas about the world, and their place in it, evolve with each encounter. Giving money is relatively easy for people who have it to give; but giving of yourself is much more demanding. When I commit to something, I only do so if I feel that I am capable of delivering the goods; there can be no letting people down. If I say I am going to be available to meet on Tuesday at 18:00, then I must be there. And when last-minute family obligations crop up, I am obliged to forfeit these in order to honour a prior social responsibility commitment. Because I generally try to balance family and public commitments, I have found that I cannot possibly accept every invitation that is extended to me.

The outreach commitments are possible only because I have been successful in my business practices; I have made enough money to be able to take time off to give to others. The programmes enrich not only the lives of others, they enrich my life too; daily, I am fortunate to encounter ordinary South Africans who are active in being responsible citizens. I learn from them, and our interaction refines my views and opinions about things. I could read a thousand books, I could study at almost any university if I so wished, but neither the books nor the academic knowledge are substitutes for the wisdom I have encountered in my meetings with people from all echelons of society.

Interaction with people challenges my perceptions, broadens my knowledge about things I have never heard of, and encourages me to consider different perspectives. I might be stubborn in the boardroom and stubborn when I take a hard line on certain family issues, but I know that while it is important to be a speaker, it is just as important to be a listener. If you are the one doing all the talking, then you are not giving yourself a chance to learn anything: I have found that to be a learner, I must first be a listener.

Chapter 20

Looking back over my career, I am able to observe the peaks and valleys, and to realise that the variations in the landscape are representative of a balanced life. Most of the highs and lows have been recalled here, but there are some poignant moments that I haven't mentioned, which have their own particular relevance.

When I started planning my first Black Like Me marketing campaign, I wanted a face that represented the "Black is Beautiful" concept. My friend and customer, Thobejane, owned a salon in Dobsonville, and one of her clients was a young singer.

"If you're looking for a face for Black Like Me, I've got just the person for you," Thobejane said.

"Okay, but I don't want just any beautiful black girl," I said. "She must have some special quality."

"I wasn't thinking of just anyone, I was thinking of Yvonne Chaka Chaka," she said. "She's really special. I could easily put you in touch, she's one of my customers."

I was delighted; Yvonne is a beautiful, positive, cheerful woman, and at the time her career was poised on the brink of greatness. Thobejane introduced me to the singer, who had just released her first record "Mr Deejay". There was no diva nonsense about her, and she graciously agreed to be the face of Black Like Me.

I was still new at marketing, and Yvonne and I still laugh at the first poster we produced. I thought it was an easy matter: I've got the girl, all I need is a photographer. I didn't have a clue about the process of producing a poster, and I had to be very careful about finances because we had so little money. When I made enquiries, I discovered that making a poster wasn't as simple as I'd thought: I'd have to hire a studio, a professional photographer, and then send the photographs for colour separation before they went to print. Because I was so broke at the time, I decided to take a shortcut and try to find my own photographer. So I phoned my contacts and managed to get hold of a photographer who worked for the *Pretoria News*; I really thought I'd hit the jackpot when he offered me the use of the *Pretoria News* studio. Poor Yvonne, we tried to do the photo shoot as tastefully as possible, but when you're doing everything on the cheap, it shows. Of course, when I look at it now, it's not the most glamorous poster, but at the time it did its job and had a positive impact on our visibility and sales. In retrospect, we should probably have waited until we had enough money to do a proper job; on the other hand, though, a big part of growing a company is exactly this kind of learning experience.

Another memorable moment involved Felicia Mabuza-Suttle, who had lived in the United States for many years and returned to South Africa after the 1994 elections; she had done so in response to Nelson Mandela's request to South Africans living abroad to return home to help rebuild the new democracy. In the mid-1990s, she started a TV show that aimed at getting ordinary South Africans of all races to engage on issues they couldn't discuss together during apartheid. *The Felicia Show* was described as "the pulse of the nation", and was featured on NBC, CBS, ABC, CNN and the BBC; its impact was reported in the *New York Times* and the *Atlanta Journal*, and it also featured in magazines such as *Constitution*, *InStyle* (SA), *Ebony*, *Essence* and *Style*, and many other international publications.

Connie and I regularly bumped into Felicia at social events, and as a result of our conversations, Connie said, "Black Like Me needs a brand ambassador, and Felicia would be perfect for the role." At this stage, Connie was in the administrative section of the company.

It sounded like an excellent idea, and we approached Felicia with the proposal. She graciously accepted the offer – a privilege that Black Like Me obviously had to pay for. But part of Felicia's motive was her desire to promote black beauty and confidence; she proved to be a huge asset to Black Like Me, and we were extremely pleased with her role in the company.

I admired Felicia not only for her beauty, but also her outspokenness. Apartheid had eroded the self-esteem of black South Africans, and Felicia showed people that, just because you're black, this doesn't mean you've got to stand back. When I speak publicly I always say that I survived because I avoided contact with white people in my formative years, thus avoiding any impairment to my dignity. I used to listen to my mother and my peers who worked in white areas, and I could see that they came back diminished – because of this, I was determined to avoid contact with white people. The point of using the Black Like Me name was to restore a sense of pride and dignity, qualities that Felicia admirably demonstrated. She was outspoken but not arrogant. To me, she was the epitome of what Black Like Me stood for. As our ambassador, Felicia featured on posters and appeared at Black Like Me functions, thereby showing her sincere involvement in the brand.

There are always people whose names don't appear in the limelight, people whose input has impact but who function behind the scenes. Beryl Baker is one such person. I met her when Nelson Mandela was about to turn eighty. I had been approached by the government to take charge of the committee that was organising Mandela's birthday celebrations, but I didn't feel ready to take on such an important international event. Beryl was on our committee, and at the time she was working with Suzanne Weil and Associates. I was impressed with her professionalism and I used to joke and say, "One day when

Suzanne's not looking, I'm going to steal you away from the company."

Then in 1999, when there was the chance of a buy-back of Black Like Me from Colgate, I knew that I'd need a strong personal assistant as I would be spending a lot of time negotiating the buy-back. So I phoned Suzanne, and after some pleasantries I asked, "I've been wondering, is Beryl still working for you?" Suzanne told me that Beryl had left, and she promised to help me trace her. I eventually made contact with Beryl and asked, "What am I going to have to do to get you to come and work for me?" Beryl laughed and told me that she was not working – I could hardly believe my luck. Beryl turned out to be everything I had hoped for, and more; she was meticulous in ensuring that all my instructions were co-ordinated, and she regularly gave me feedback on all events that related to Black Like Me. I depended very much on this wonderful woman who was the daughter of political activists who had left South Africa when she was still young; she had returned in the early 1990s, when exiles were allowed to return to the country.

Only two years later, in 2001, Beryl discovered she had cancer; it was a terrible blow to everyone who knew and loved her. While she was in hospital undergoing treatment, Black Like Me was in the process of refurbishing and swapping offices. Beryl's office was next door to mine, and the staff relocated Beryl's office to another part of the building. When she came back from hospital, she accused the staff of trying to work her out of the company, and it was very difficult to reassure her that this was not the case. How I regret our insensitivity; that we hadn't considered her need for stability when everything else in her life was uncertain. Beryl was in her early fifties when she passed away – a dynamic, strong-willed person. We had a very good provident fund for her, which provided for her teenage daughter. But, of course, no amount of money ever replaces a mother.

Whenever Connie and I talk about Beryl, I say, "She went too soon, she deserved to see what we achieved." I have told Connie many times that, apart from her, Beryl is the one person who deserved to enjoy the company's success.

Another dear friend we lost to cancer in 2008 was Tom Henry, who had been such an important mentor to me when he was CEO of Stocks. As with Beryl, Connie and I miss his presence immensely. Fortunately, though, I haven't lost all the people with whom I've enjoyed special relationships – and one who has meant much to me is Akhter Deshmukh. In 2005 I was growing increasingly concerned about inconsistent financial reporting from one of the companies I'd bought. Shane suggested that I approach Akhter Deshmukh to do a forensic analysis of the company. Within two days, Akhter had discovered the source of the problem, and as a result of his findings we decided to disinvest, and the company was forced to buy us out. I was impressed by Akhter's astute financial capabilities, and he joined Leswikeng in 2005 as our Chief Financial Officer. Ever since, he has been an invaluable member of our team, but he has also become a firm friend.

I am not usually one to look back, because when you look back you cannot see the opportunities that lie ahead of you. So I will return to my story, where I have tried to discover why I managed to succeed and why my brother did not. This quest is linked to the question whether the younger generation in our country will or will not make it in the future. It all comes down to the events and experiences, but especially the choices, which shape our lives. Perhaps if I divide people into two groups I will be able, in some way, to identify what it is that separates achievers from the rest, especially those who fall by the wayside.

Faith has underpinned my self-confidence – faith in God and faith in myself and my own abilities. Defeatists say, "Nobody is listening!" or "I don't believe in God", but what they are really saying is, "I'm not listening to myself", and "I feel as if God has abandoned me". A healthy self-esteem and the willingness to take advantage of opportunities almost guarantee the achievement of a person's goals. Achievers believe in themselves and in their abilities, while defeatists do not believe that they have any ability or skill whatsoever.

In the earliest days of my career, I had a robust sense of purpose. When I wanted to move away from a salaried position into a sales position, I knew that I had to be mobile. When I wanted to purchase my first car, I worked as if there were 48 hours in a day, and in this way I saved enough for a small deposit. While I was saving, my fellow employees were squandering their salaries on luxury items or trendy clothes, or on dice games or horse-racing, or on loose women in shebeens. While Connie and I lived in the tiny Zozo, we saved whatever we could put aside, and at night we shared our dreams about making a bright future for ourselves. Pobane and I both had a vision for our lives, but Pobane's unskilled status meant that he had to fight every day to get a job ahead of a skilled worker, making it extremely stressful to keep his family clothed and fed; his lack of higher education and diminished circumstances resulted in his getting into a survival mode that was difficult – though not impossible, I have to say – to escape. The business of survival is so overwhelming that it becomes impossible to focus on anything else; it slows one down, keeps things stagnant, so that it becomes almost impossible to change direction, resulting, eventually, in defeat. I, on the other hand, wanted to achieve things, I knew what type of lifestyle I wanted for my family, and I knew the absolute commitment and self-sacrifice it would take to make the journey towards my destination. A strong sense of who I was and what I wanted helped me to achieve my goal of buying a car; but in Pobane's case, a diminished sense of self, as well as purpose, defeated him.

When I was growing up, I had to make my own way. It was

necessary to insulate myself against a negative environment so that I could remain focused in unsympathetic surroundings. I kept my eye on the ball, and this helped me to ignore the problems and seek solutions.

Robert F Kennedy once said that defeatists ask "Why?", and achievers ask "Why not?". I've sat in many a shebeen listening to a melancholy drunk wailing about the unfairness of the world, "Why, why, why?" These defeatists bemoan everything, from why they haven't won the Lotto to why their electricity was cut off. A persistently pessimistic, self-pitying attitude removes people from the reality of their situation. By blaming God, or their awful employers, or their unmotivated children, they don't have to face up to their own responsibilities. Their eternal complaining puts the responsibility on someone else's shoulders, and their failure to rise to life's challenges bogs them down in self-pity. Achievers buck the system, the status quo, and attempts at control that frustrate them. They not only challenge the world's perception of them, but also demand more from themselves.

When I decided to leave SuperKurl, Leon Thompson said, "Why? You're earning a lot of money, your life is comfortable." After I left, he was still asking "Why?", wallowing in the regret of having lost a key staff member. This negative question dragged him into a pit of recrimination. But my "Why not?" buoyed my spirits and took me far beyond what I imagined I was able to do. I had no business management experience, I had no formal business education – and I had never expanded my limited skills. But when I started Black Like Me I was forced to exceed my limits, and in the first few months I learnt how to mix formulas, how to market products, and how to negotiate with suppliers. If I'd been content to operate within the confines of the law, I would have stagnated; instead, I rebelled and developed both the company and myself. Every time anyone asked me questions like, "Why should we give you this permit?", "Why should we employ you?", "Why do you need a telephone?", I ignored them and said, "Why not?" This retort has always kept me on my toes, forcing me to reach higher each time.

Achievers work to a master plan, and this enables them to be in control of their emotions. A healthy emotional state is important for any businessperson who has to interact with other people and keep focused on the bigger picture; it is imperative to keep emotion out of the business arena. When Pobane died, I felt numb. I wanted to feel more, and I thought I should feel more. He was my brother, and I loved him; but I had never really known him because we were both, in our own ways, too busy trying to make a living to satisfy our domestic and emotional needs.

As a result, most of my life has been occupied with putting one foot in front of the other to achieve each of my goals systematically. Taking responsibility for one's life does not always allow one the luxury of emotion – though this does not mean that one does not feel anger, disappointment, frustration, or even elation. What it does mean is that indulging these feelings makes no positive contribution whatsoever to one's life. One has to move on.

If I had allowed my longing for my mother's warm embrace to overwhelm me, then I would not have had the will or found the strength to steal wood to keep me warm on bitter winter nights. If I had allowed the cruel comments at Pobane's funeral to upset me, I would not have had the strength to be a support to my mother and sisters, who gave in to their grief. Giving rein to my emotions would have depleted the energy reserves that I needed when Black Like Me was just a fledgling company.

Throughout my life, Connie has been my anchor, though there have been times in the boardroom when she has reacted emotionally to decisions that have gone against her wishes and plans. If I had allowed my strategy to be derailed by her tears of frustration or disappointment, I would not have been able to keep the interests of the company at the forefront of my mind. It is not that Connie's ideas or ambitions for the company were not good, it is just that I did not think they were right at the time. When she wanted to launch a cosmetic line, much as I admired her innovation, I felt that the product range was not complementary to our core business focus at the time. So I rejected her idea, even though I agreed in principle with a longer-term plan for a cosmetics line. It was hard to see Connie upset, but it would have been far worse to lose Black Like Me because of a wrong business decision based on emotional support of my wife. It is not always easy to be firm, but it has always been necessary in ensuring success.

I operate on gut feeling. But gut feel is not an emotional reaction; it is an instinctual one. When you have been in business for as long as I have, you quickly become attuned to ideas, programmes and strategies that make good business sense and you cannot weaken that intuition by allowing your emotions to get the upper hand. Emotion wipes logic off the game-board, and you cannot jeopardise the life of a company and the livelihoods of the people who work for it by allowing emotions to triumph. I have had to keep cool when caustic comments from detractors have threatened to derail my plans; in such circumstances, I have fought hard not to allow my emotional guard to slip, as I instinctively knew that this would jeopardise my ability to provide for my family and myself.

All this is not to say that I have not made mistakes, or that I have no regrets; there is surely not a man alive who can honestly make such a claim. However, I have never allowed mistakes or regrets to keep me shackled to a safe path where opportunities may be hidden from view. There is no room for over-cautiousness or the desire for safety in entrepreneurship. Entrepreneurs are, by definition, risk-takers; over-cautious circumspection kills the vitality that lies at the heart of entrepreneurship, its opportunistic impulse.

Because defeatists continually lament the failures in their

lives, they usually lurch from one failure to another. They use past failures to justify their refusal to take risks, and so they trap themselves in the blame game and are unable to lift themselves out of the morass and into a new venture. Achievers seldom consider the possibility of failure, because their minds are utterly focused on their visions and plans for the future. When I sold Black Like Me to Colgate-Palmolive, I did so because I believed that my company's objectives would be enabled by Colgate's strength. But the opposite proved to be true: Colgate suffocated Black Like Me. However, I do not consider the sale a failure; I see it as a learning experience. I remained committed to the pursuit of the company's goals, and subsequent to the buy-back from Colgate, I achieved those goals.

If I'd been a defeatist, the fire at the Black Like Me premises would have been the perfect excuse for me to throw up my hands in the wake of all the ugly rumours that surfaced at the time. But I refused to give in to the crisis; instead, I turned to Louis and said, "This won't get us down – it's just another challenge, and we'll get on top of it." Not once did I ask, "Why is this happening to me?" I instinctively knew that becoming self-absorbed would demand too much energy. In spite of all the odds, I had to show a dogged determination to my employees, I had to make important decisions, and take proactive steps to literally rebuild the company from the ground up. So I persevered, taking one step at a time in rebuilding Black Like Me.

The longer I live, the more convinced I am that education does not stop when you step outside a formal learning institution: education is an ongoing process. Achievers seek out opportunities to acquire and learn the skills they need. I could not complete my university studies, but that did not stop me from listening to the ideas of people I met during my working experience, and eventually trying out some of those ideas myself. Many of my schoolmates at GaRamotse went to school merely to conform; they failed to see the real purpose of education –

a springboard to achieving one's goals. When I started reading books – biographies, autobiographies and personal profiles, in particular – I realised that the information I needed to improve my skills was there for the taking. I did not have to attend university; I simply had to read about people who had educated themselves, and who were willing to share their experiences and skills with me in the pages of a book. Defeatists bemoan the lack of learning opportunities or access to them, believing that education opportunities exist only in formal institutions. My experience has shown that education in its broadest terms is developed by interaction with others, by engaging with ideas, by educating oneself through reading or mentorships. These things mostly cost nothing; books, for example, can be borrowed from a library for free.

Some people work for their money, while others make their money work for them. Few people realise the true value of money. Most people throughout the world treat money as if it is something that is earned in order to be spent; they spend their money on designer clothing with trendy labels, or on fine furniture or luxury cars – they feel they have worked hard for their money and so they spend it to make themselves feel good. But there is another way of feeling good about money – by making it work for you.

Judicious investment makes money grow, thereby helping investors to accumulate the wealth necessary to afford the lifestyle they aspire to; wise investments also help people to avoid incurring debt. A responsible approach to money has nothing to do with one's position on the economic ladder – rather, it is an attitude that one develops. We have all read stories about people who have lived modestly and accumulated millions because of prudent spending habits and sensible investment practices.

Achievers are by nature people who try to find solutions to problems. My entire village lacked exposure to whites-only pursuits; we had no cinemas, no dance halls and no proper sports fields, but I refused to surrender to my circumstances. I played soccer with the rest of the kids on the dusty patch of ground that was GaRamotse's soccer field, but I wanted more than this. I also wanted to play tennis, so I ignored my abhorrence of the policemen who intimidated us and learnt to play at the Hammanskraal Police Training College tennis courts.

I told myself that I had the opportunity of learning to play a fun game normally denied to township kids, so I took full advantage of the situation and solved the problem of a lack of facilities. Tennis is a great social game, but it also taught me a useful skill that I later transferred to my business dealings: it taught me about strategy. In the game of tennis, players use different strategies to gain advantage and to exploit their opponent's weaknesses with the purpose of winning more points and eventually winning game, set and the match. Strategy consists of the overall plan, and tactics are the detailed manoeuvres in each game, whereby players work towards winning the set, and eventually achieving their overall plan – winning the match.

Each tennis player develops a specific style of play, focusing on individual strengths to beat an opponent. A baseline player plays from the back of the tennis court, favouring ground strokes rather than approaching the net; a volley player works best at the net, hitting hard shots that put pressure on the opponent; and all-court players have a good balance between these playing styles. But the most important aspect of tennis is learning to read your opponent and to play according to their weakness. These principles also apply in business. When I bought a share in the ferrochrome smelter in 2002, I played on the other party's weakness in order to negotiate a good deal for myself. I knew exactly why Samancor was dragging their feet over doing a deal with their ex-staff – they didn't fit the BEE profile. And long before this, during the Black Like Me days, in negotiating with suppliers I had to strategise carefully. With some suppliers I negotiated like a volley player, getting up close and putting pressure on them, while with others I negotiated from the baseline, proceeding cautiously, especially if the supplier was likely to become aggressive.

The key to being an achiever is using every possible experience to enhance your business. When you play chess, for example, you have to think two moves ahead of your opponent, pre-empting the person's moves. Incorporating these kinds of skills into your business is useful and rewarding. Achievers seek solutions from a diverse range of possibilities, and they don't settle for second best.

Successful people are a combination of the talents they are born with and those they learn from their environment. I had an economically disadvantaged start, but fortunately my care-givers were people who encouraged and nurtured me, helping me to become a productive person. My youthful interaction with people generally involved discussing politics, religion, community issues – even music. Everyone was allowed to participate, and this created a thirst for more interaction and information. I was an inquisitive child; I wanted to learn. I listened to stories of triumph and tragedy, power and subjugation, and through these stories I made choices regarding the kind of life I wanted to live. My brother had had an almost identical childhood, with the additional benefit of knowing our father; Pobane had access to the same education that I did, and there were fewer demands placed on him in terms of supporting our family from a young age. I refused to work for white people; Pobane, on the other hand, worked for anyone who paid him. I decided to complete my high school education; Pobane decided that it was a waste of time. The nurturing we received was almost identical, our fighting spirit may even have been similar, but the one area in which we differed greatly was that of choice – Pobane and I chose different paths.

By what yardstick does one measure the success of an individual's life? My mother thought I was a success when I had enough income to marry Connie; Connie considered me highly successful when I bought a car and started Black Like Me; my friends considered my lifestyle to be the outward sign of my success; and today the media rate me as a success in terms of my board memberships and company assets. But this is merely financial prosperity; these things do not measure the real success of having lived a good life.

To me, genuine success has a social dimension. In my own case, it has meant engaging meaningfully with my family, friends and colleagues; it has meant enjoying a game of tennis with Connie, spending a pleasant afternoon with Khensani and Rhulani, enjoying a holiday in Dubai with my sisters and their families, poring over old family photographs on a Sunday afternoon, or relaxing in the clubhouse after a game of golf at Killarney with Louis. Whether success is measured on a social, personal or professional scale, its significance ultimately lies not so much in one's personal achievements, but rather in one's relationships with other people, especially one's family and friends.

Chapter 21

I have often had to be absent from home, when work has demanded more of me than seemed fair, but I have always had the luxury of home and family to return to. My family comprises not only Connie and Khensani and Rhulani – it also includes my extended family, my sisters, in-laws, nieces and nephews, friends, and even some colleagues. Without these people to share it with, my success would be worth nothing at all. Losing my father at a young age, having a mother who was absent for most of my formative years, and losing my brother Pobane, have meant that I take no one at all for granted. I am very grateful for the time I was able to spend with my grandparents – cooking pap for my maternal granny, and walking and talking with my paternal grandfather as he wheeled his bicycle along the sandy roads of Hammanskraal.

During the latter part of her life, my mother was able to spend a lot of time with Connie and me. I think back on her with much affection, but I also remember her stubbornness, especially when it came to smoking. We all tried very hard to explain the health risks, but she would have none of it. "Your father sang in the church choir, and he never smoked a day in his life. And look what happened – he died when he was still a young man!" She refused to heed our warnings and often referred to the longevity of my granny, who had lived to the age of 96; my mother took it for granted that she'd make old bones too – but this was not to be. She was only in her seventies when she took ill and I sent her to our dear friend, Dr Komati, in Pretoria. He was a specialist physician, and discovered that my mother was in the advanced stages of lung cancer. I will never forget his words, "I'm sorry to tell you that your mother is at a stage where not even chemotherapy will help."

As ill as she was, however, my mother continued to smoke, and though I didn't want to be harsh on her, at times it was hard to restrain myself. I hated the fact that she was dying because of something she was doing to herself. Shortly after the diagnosis, she moved in with our family. We took her for regular check-ups, and I recall one occasion when Dr Komati reached across for her hand, but my mother clenched her fist and refused to open her palm. With great patience, Dr Komati slowly unfurled her fingers, and there, clutched in her palm, was a cigarette. She tried to hide her smoking from us, but eventually Dr Komati said to us, "It's no use trying to stop her, and in any case, it doesn't matter any more whether she smokes or not. It's best to leave her in peace."

Six months after she was diagnosed with cancer, my mother died; in accordance with her wishes, we buried her in GaRamotse, next to my father. It was 1996, and with both parents gone, another chapter in my life had ended. I am grateful that my mother died owning a house of her own, and that she had at last enjoyed the right to vote, and, most importantly that she'd been able to welcome our daughter, Khensani, into the world, and to spend a little time with her. My younger sister, Nancy, bears a remarkable likeness to my mother, and whenever we spend time together, I am happy to be reminded of my mother.

Many people say that when the matriarch dies, the family disintegrates, but this was not the case with us. When I book a family holiday, it usually includes my entire family and as well as some friends and their children. This is because I want to spend all my leisure time with the people I love most. I don't want Khensani and Rhulani to know their father mainly through newspaper reports and TV programmes on entrepreneurship; I don't want my family to know me only as the uncle who pays school fees. I want them to know me as a father, a brother, an uncle, a husband, a friend. I want them to know the Herman who can't help dancing whenever his favourite music plays; the Herman who wants his whole family to see the White House, instead of looking enviously at our holiday photographs. "It's no fun if you can't share it," I always say.

In spite of my heavy work schedule, I try to spend as much time as I can with Connie and the children, though during the week Connie manages to spend more time with Khensani and Rhulani than I do. She makes a point of picking up them up from school and regularly takes them on outings – often by themselves – where they can enjoy lunch together and chat or watch a movie. Some weekends we play a round of golf together at Killarney or River Club, or else the four of us play a game of tennis. We also regularly enjoy dinner together at a restaurant, although the children's preferences are not always the same as ours – they still shout "Spur!" when I offer to take them out. But I enjoy the casual lack of fuss at the steakhouse, so I don't really mind; I have enough black-tie events without having to dress up for dinner with my wife and kids.

But there are times when I like to escape and just have a day out with the guys. Then I'm usually to be found on the Killarney golf course with my old friend, Louis, and Noel Machingawuta and Alex Darko. I play off an 18 handicap, and I just love the game. I'm often a bit of a joker, and sometimes I think my golfing companions would like me to be a bit more serious – but my whole work week is serious and usually stressful, and golf is an opportunity to relax.

In spite of my great love of music, I have never learnt to play an instrument other than the drums I banged on as a child in GaRamotse. In the late 1980s, when Connie and I bought the house in Heatherdale, a wooden-cased organ was included in the purchase. This beautiful organ travelled with us from

Heatherdale and it stood in the formal lounge of our current home in Atholl for many years. I'd always intended to learn to play the organ, mainly because I love the sound of it; but it also brought back the past, reminding me of the music I enjoyed in the late 1960s, when the organ was a popular instrument. Unfortunately, though, I never seemed to find the time to take even a single lesson – and I never considered giving up a game of golf in favour of music lessons.

Towards the end of 2010, though, I took a firm decision – to learn to play the piano. A new Yamaha Clavinova piano replaced the organ in our living room and I started lessons, and in just over three months I was able to play most of my favourite tunes without the sheet music. It has been a wonderful experience, and I now spend many happy hours making music at the piano keyboard – a welcome relief from sitting in front of a computer keyboard. One can learn a new skill at any stage of one's life, as I have discovered. And while not everyone has the resources or the time, it is probably fair to say that our only real limitations are the ones we construct in our minds.

My quest at the beginning of this book was to find out what got me to where I am today, and why my life has been so blessed. In the end, I have to say that it is a combination of good decisions and choices – and the one thing that all successful people have in common: damn good luck.